CAGE BIRD Identifier

CAGE BIRD
Identifier

By HELMUT BECHTEL

With photographs by the author

STERLING PUBLISHING CO., Inc., New York

Oak Tree Press Co., Ltd. London & Sydney

OTHER BOOKS OF INTEREST

Tropical Fish Identifier
Colorful Mineral Identifier
How to Raise and Train Pigeons
Bird Life (for young people)
Pigeon Racing

Translated by Kenneth T. Dutfield

The publisher would like to thank Dr. Helmut Adler of the
American Museum of Natural History, and D. H. S. Risdon
of the Tropical Bird Gardens, Rode (near Bath), England, for
invaluable assistance in the preparation of this edition.

Published by Sterling Publishing Co, Inc.
Two Park Avenue, New York 10016
Distributed in Australia by Oak Tree Press Co., Ltd.,
P.O. Box 34, Brickfield Hill, Sydney 2000, N.S.W.
Distributed in the United Kingdom
by Ward Lock Ltd., 116 Baker Street, London W 1
Based on the original work "Bunte Welt der Stuben-
vögel" by Helmut Bechtel, © 1971 Franckh'sche
Verlagshandlung, Stuttgart, W. Germany.
Printed in Hong Kong
All rights reserved
Library of Congress Catalog Card No.: 72-81049
ISBN 0–8069-3718–1   UK 7061– 2385–9
3719 –X

COVER PICTURE

POPULAR NAMES: **Red-headed Barbet; Red-breasted Barbet**

SCIENTIFIC NAME: *Eubocco bourcierii*

FAMILY: Capitonidae (Barbets)

About 7 different sub-species of the bird reproduced on the cover (the Red-headed Barbet) live in the dense undergrowth of the tropical and subtropical forests of Central America, Colombia, Ecuador and Peru. These birds generally reach a length of $6\frac{1}{2}''$ (17 cm). The Red-headed Barbet lives mainly on wild fruits and insects. Only the male bird has the red head and red breast plumage. This Barbet nests in tree holes; the young birds—2 to 4 of them—leave their eggs after 14 days.

If you keep one (or more) of these birds, remember that the Red-headed Barbet is sensitive to cold and dampness.

FOOD: This bird should be fed with packaged soft food, meal-worms, shredded meat, and fruit.

BREEDING: The Red-headed Barbet can seldom be successfully bred in captivity.

INCHES

CENTIMETRES

MILLIMETRES

LINEAR CONVERSIONS

The linear system has been used to specify lengths and dimensions in this book. Conversions into the metric scale are given below.

in.	cm.	in.	cm.	in.	cm.
$\frac{1}{4}$	0.6	$2\frac{1}{2}$	6.3	7	17.8
$\frac{1}{2}$	1.3	3	7.6	8	20.3
1	2.5	4	10.2	9	22.9
$1\frac{1}{2}$	3.8	5	12.7	10	25.4
2	5.1	6	15.2	12	30.5

CONTENTS

INTRODUCTION

THIS POCKET GUIDEBOOK has been written for amateurs who keep birds in cages or aviaries and also for bird-lovers and those who are fond of visiting zoos. There are so many kinds of cage birds for sale today that almost everyone can find one to suit his tastes—and, happily, the birds reach us, thanks to fast transport by air, in better condition than they often did in the old days. From the vast number of available cage birds, we have chosen those that thrive best in captivity and are most popular, but we have also included a few of the less common and more "difficult" species.

Everyone who keeps cage birds naturally does his best to look after his feathered pets with as much consideration as possible for their natural needs, to keep a careful watch over them, and—if possible—to breed from them. Remember that a bird-cage cannot possibly be too big! Every bird needs enough freedom of movement to make it feel contented. The smaller the cage, the more likely it is that quarrels will break out between the inhabitants. Correct "population planning" in an aviary containing different species of birds will prevent losses. "Original," highly ornamental cages are often prisons that birds hate having to live in. Keeping a single bird—with a few exceptions—is cruelty to animals. Parrots, for example, are very sociable creatures when they can live in freedom. Unfiltered sunlight is a vital necessity for most birds. Even window panes reduce the essential ultra-violet radiation in light.

The experimental cross-breeding of related species of birds, although it is so popular, is less important—unless it is an important scientific experiment—than the propagation of pure species. This is particularly true of rare birds and of those threatened with extinction.

The birds illustrated in this book are in private ownership or can be seen in many zoological gardens. They have been photographed either in their aviaries or in a special photography-cage. The use of longer focal lengths (7" and 15¾"; 18 cm and 40 cm) in the Leicaflex camera made it possible to photograph the birds without disturbing them.

Family and Sub-family Chart

Falcon

Pheasant

Dove

Barbet

Hummingbird

Parrot

Hoopoe

Toucan

Pitta

11

Cotinga

Leafbird

Bulbul

Babbler

Sunbird

Thrush

Waxwing

White-eye

Bunting

Cardinal

Tanager

Icterid

Finch

Weaverbird

Weaverfinch

Starling

Crow

POPULAR NAMES: **Coppersmith; Crimson-breasted Barbet**

SCIENTIFIC NAME: *Megalaima haemacephala*

FAMILY: Capitonidae (Barbets)

India, Burma, Thailand, Cambodia, Laos, Vietnam, Malaysia, and the Philippines are the home of this 6½″ (roughly 16 cm) bird. The call of the Coppersmith sounds like someone's hammering on metal: hence the bird's name. In its native haunts, this "hammering" is one of the most familiar of all bird-calls. The Coppersmith lives in the forests of its native countries, but it also visits towns and villages, showing no fear of human beings. It feels at home in the banyan and other *Ficus* trees. Fruit and berries are its chief food. The bird also captures flying termites. The Coppersmith prefers a concealed hole in the bough of a tree to incubate its eggs in and also as a resting-place for the night. It quickly becomes tame in captivity.

FOOD: In captivity, berries and other fruits. Also, insectivorous food.

Coppersmith

POPULAR NAMES: **Toucan Barbet; Toucan-billed Barbet**

SCIENTIFIC NAME: *Semnornis ramphastinus*

FAMILY: Capitonidae (Barbets)

This particularly colorful Barbet—about 8" (20 cm) long—comes from Ecuador and Colombia. The Toucan Barbet lives in pairs, frequenting mountain forests at elevations between 8,000 and 10,000 feet (between 2,500 and 3,000 metres) above sea level. It lives in tree holes and feeds chiefly on soft fruit and insects.

FOOD AND CARE: In captivity, soft fruit such as bananas and grapes; berries; greenstuff; and mealworms, ants' eggs and the like. As the Toucan Barbet lives in quite high regions of the Andes, remember that this bird is sensitive to heat—and to cold as well.

BREEDING: The Toucan Barbet is a peaceable bird when kept in an aviary, but it has not yet bred in captivity.

Toucan Barbet

This falcon, which is never more than about 7″ in height (18 cm), lives mainly on the warm slopes of the Himalayas, but spends the winter farther south. It is a sociable bird and hunts its prey—insects, mice and small birds—in the same way as the big falcons do: by rapid swoops. It builds its nest in hollow trees. The Indian Falconet will feel really comfortable only in a spacious cage that will give it enough room to spread its wings.

FOOD: To thrive in captivity, it needs not only meat and insects but also somewhat large, living animals to feed on. Therefore, the tastes of the Indian Falconet will probably make many bird-lovers hesitate before deciding to keep one of these beautiful birds.

BREEDING: A nesting box will suit the Indian Falconet as a place to sleep in. It rarely breeds in captivity.

Indian Falconet

POPULAR NAME: **Chinese Painted Quail**
SCIENTIFIC NAME: *Coturnix chinensis*
FAMILY: Phasianidae (Pheasants)

Less than 5″ (12 cm) long, this bird comes from India, southern China, Indo-China, Celebes [Sulawesi], the Philippines, and the Molucca Islands. A monogamous bird living in open country, the Chinese Painted Quail finds its food on the ground—in the form of seeds, insects, and worms. The nest-hollow, concealed by tall grass, contains 4 to 6 eggs which are incubated for 16 to 18 days. It is friendly toward other birds, although not to its rivals, and will become quite tame.

FOOD AND CARE: The Chinese Quail's diet should be varied—grain enriched with greens, mealworms, and other such things. The bird also needs sand to scratch and clean itself in.

BREEDING: It must have a piece of grassy ground as a nesting place.

Chinese Painted Quail

POPULAR NAME: **Californian Quail**
SCIENTIFIC NAME: *Lophortyx californica*
FAMILY: Phasianidae (Pheasants)

About 9½″ (24 cm) long, this bird is at home in the west of North America. Except during the breeding season, these ground-dwelling birds assemble in great flocks; during breeding time they live in pairs. Their varied food is similar to that of the Chinese Painted Quail. The Californian Quail lays 12 to 20 eggs, from which the youngsters emerge after 23 days.

FOOD: When the Californian Quail is rearing its young, its food should include plenty of meat.

BREEDING: This bird will breed if kept in a sufficiently large aviary, but it does not like dampness.

Californian Quail

POPULAR NAME: **Diamond Dove**
SCIENTIFIC NAME: *Geopelia cuneata*
FAMILY: Columbidae (Pigeons and Doves)

Central Australia is the native territory of this bird, which reaches a length of only 7″ to 7½″ (18 to 19 cm). Living in country containing scattered bushes and clumps of trees, this bird prefers grass seeds above all other food. The Diamond Dove builds its nest near the ground in dense scrub; the clutch never consists of more than 2 eggs. The eggs are incubated for 17 days, and the young birds leave the nest 10 days later.

FOOD: Grain and a good packaged soft food.

BREEDING: The Diamond Dove will breed in captivity, hatching its eggs in a small basket or wooden box—possibly several times a year. It is not a troublesome bird to keep, although it is sensitive to winter cold.

Diamond Dove

POPULAR NAME: **Moluccan Cockatoo**
SCIENTIFIC NAME: *Cacatua moluccensis*
FAMILY: Psittacidae (Parrots)
SUB-FAMILY: Cacatuinae (Cockatoos)

About 19½″ to 20″ long (50 cm), this bird lives in the forests of the islands of Ceram, Saparua, and Haruku (some of the eastern Moluccas of Indonesia). Occasionally it looks for its chief food—fruit and large seeds—in cultivated land. The Moluccan Cockatoo builds its nest in tree holes, with the hen laying 3 to 5 eggs. It is regarded as one of the most attractive of the cockatoos. When tame it hardly uses its screeching call and is a highly talented talker. It is a sought-after household pet in its homeland, too.

FOOD: Grain and fruit, as varied as possible.

BREEDING: Unfortunately it has not yet been possible to breed this beautiful cockatoo in captivity.

Moluccan Cockatoo

POPULAR NAMES: **Bare-eyed Cockatoo; Little Corella**
SCIENTIFIC NAME: *Cacatua sanguinea*
FAMILY Psittacidae (Parrots)
SUB-FAMILY: Cacatuinae (Cockatoos)

One of the friendliest of all cockatoos and one of
the most gifted talkers, this bird is to be found at
home in the semi-deserts of the interior of Australia. The Bare-eyed Cockatoo (14"; 35 cm) lives
sociably, like all of the cockatoos. The birds often
form enormous flocks and are particularly fond of
gathering in places where water is nearby.

The Bare-eyed Cockatoo is one of the friendliest
of all cockatoos and one of the most gifted talkers.
It incubates its eggs—not more than 3—in hollow
trees.

FOOD: In captivity, this bird should be given the
same kind of food as the Moluccan Cockatoo. If
supplied with fresh twigs, it will be less tempted to
gnaw its cage and perch.

BREEDING: Unlike the Moluccan Cockatoo, this
bird will breed if kept in a sufficiently big aviary.
A hollow tree trunk or big nesting box placed in
the aviary will serve as a suitable place for the
eggs to be hatched in.

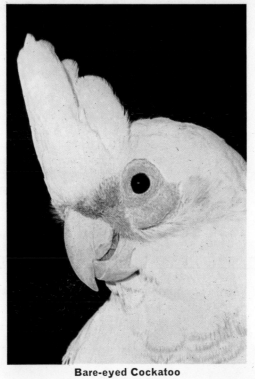

Bare-eyed Cockatoo

POPULAR NAME: **Lesser Sulphur-crested Cockatoo**
SCIENTIFIC NAME: *Cacatua sulphurea*
FAMILY: Psittacidae (Parrots)
SUB-FAMILY: Cacatuinae (Cockatoos)

This Cockatoo, which attains a length of nearly 14″ (almost 35 cm), comes from Celebes [Sulawesi] and other islands in Indonesia. It has much in common with the rather larger Sulphur-crested Cockatoo (*Cacatua galerita*). The Lesser Sulphur-crested Cockatoo looks for fruit, its chief food, in the tops of the forest trees, but also visits cornfields. It nests in tree holes and forms big flocks. The young birds leave their eggs after 4 weeks and are fledged 3 months later.

FOOD: In captivity, sunflower and hemp seeds, wheat, corn, apples, berries, nuts and greenstuff.

BREEDING: In captivity, breeding has proved repeatedly successful when the Lesser Sulphur-crested Cockatoo's nesting boxes are hung up high. The Lesser Sulphur-crested Cockatoo is docile and quickly becomes quite tame.

Lesser Sulphur-crested Cockatoo

POPULAR NAME: **Leadbeater's Cockatoo**
SCIENTIFIC NAME: *Cacatua leadbeateri*
FAMILY: Psittacidae (Parrots)
SUB-FAMILY: Cacatuinae (Cockatoos)

Leadbeater's Cockatoo may well be proud of its distinctive and beautiful crest of feathers. (All the cockatoos have a raisable crest.) There are several sub-species of this bird, and they live in the semi-deserts of central Australia: usually where there is water not far away.

The maximum size of this bird is somewhat less than 16″ (40 cm). Leadbeater's Cockatoo looks for its food—seeds, bulbs, tubers and berries—chiefly on the ground. It makes its nest in hollow trees.

FOOD: This bird lives on the same kind of food as the Lesser Sulphur-crested Cockatoo. When Leadbeater's Cockatoo is bringing up its youngsters, however, food should be augmented with sprouting grain, crackers and bread-crusts soaked in milk.

Leadbeater's Cockatoo

POPULAR NAMES: **Cockatiel; Cockateel**
SCIENTIFIC NAME: *Nymphicus hollandicus*
FAMILY: Psittacidae (Parrots)
SUB-FAMILY: Psittacinae (True Parrots)

Just where the Cockatiel belongs in the bird-classification system is a disputed question; some ornithologists place it near the cockatoos (it has a raisable crest). The Cockatiel lives in the savannas and grasslands of central Australia and, like the Budgerigar, it roams in great flocks—following the varying supply of food—from district to district. The Cockatiel can do a great deal of damage in cultivated land. It lays 4 to 7 eggs in tree holes; the eggs are incubated by both parents alternately. Adult birds reach a length of 12″ to 14″ (30 to 35 cm).

FOOD: Like that of the other long-tailed parakeets.

BREEDING: One of the most peaceable and easy-to-please of all parrots, the Cockatiel will readily breed in captivity.

Cockatiel

POPULAR NAMES: **Rosella Parakeet; Red Rosella**
SCIENTIFIC NAME: *Platycercus eximius*
FAMILY: Psittacidae (Parrots)
SUB-FAMILY: Psittacinae (True Parrots)

Southeastern Australia and the island of Tasmania are the home country of this long-tailed parakeet. It comes in several sub-species, all of which live in open country interspersed with groups of trees and dense thickets of scrub. The average size of the bird is $12\frac{1}{2}''$ (32 cm). It dotes on river areas, but often also visits gardens and parks. The Red Rosella feeds on grass seed, fruits, greenstuff, and the flowers of trees. If, as occasionally happens, it finds its way into cornfields or orchards, it is chased away by the farmer or land-owner. The Red Rosella makes its nest in tree holes, with the hen laying 4 to 9 eggs.

FOOD: Canary-grass seed [the seeds of the *Phalaris canariensis* or of any species of *Lepidium* grass], sunflower and millet seeds, oats, fruit, berries and greenstuff.

BREEDING: It will readily breed in an aviary.

Rosella Parakeet

POPULAR NAMES: **Stanley's Parakeet; Yellow-cheeked Rosella**
SCIENTIFIC NAME: *Platycercus icterotis*
FAMILY: Psittacidae (Parrots)
SUB-FAMILY: Psittacinae (True Parrots)

The southwest of Australia is the homeland of this 11″ (28 cm) long-tailed parakeet. The scattered trees of the grassy plains are the natural habitat of Stanley's Parakeet, although it makes its way also into farmland (but is not welcomed there) and into gardens, and shows no fear of human beings. It feeds on seeds, greenstuff, and fruit. Stanley's Parakeet makes its nest preferably in natural holes in eucalyptus trees, the hen laying 3 to 6 eggs. The young birds quit the eggs after 20 days and fly away from the nest a month later.

FOOD: Like that of the other long-tailed parakeets.

BREEDING: Stanley's Parakeet breeds in captivity.

Stanley's Parakeet

POPULAR NAMES: **Splendid Parakeet; Scarlet-chested Parrot**
SCIENTIFIC NAME: *Neophema splendida*
FAMILY: Psittacidae (Parrots)
SUB-FAMILY: Psittacinae (True Parrots)

It was believed for a long time that this 8½" (22 cm) Australian long-tailed parakeet was extinct, as its cherished haunts are in wild and remote places. Moreover, it is a nomadic creature, another reason why it is seldom seen. The Splendid Parakeet is a timid bird, living in pairs or in small groups. Feeding mainly on seeds, they roam those districts where there is abundant scrub and grass. The female is less brightly colored than the male (illustrated). The Splendid Parakeet lays 3 to 5 eggs in a tree hole and incubates them for 20 days.

FOOD: Like that of the Rosella Parakeet.

BREEDING: Fortunately this pet can be relied on to breed even in captivity, so that, although the wild bird is rarely seen, the Splendid Parakeet is often on sale.

Splendid Parakeet

POPULAR NAMES: **Budgerigar; Parakeet**
SCIENTIFIC NAME: *Melopsittacus undulatus*
FAMILY: Psittacidae (Parrots)
SUB-FAMILY: Psittacinae (True Parrots)

About 8″ long (20 cm), this bird belongs, like all of the parrots shown on pages 36–41, to the long-tailed-parakeet group. It lives in the interior of Australia, where—outside the period of nest care—it makes long journeys; this is why in some districts Budgerigars may appear in great numbers and then be almost entirely absent for years at a time. The Budgerigar lives mainly in grasslands having scattered trees. For in these places it can find enough of its preferred food—mainly grass seed—and tree holes to make its nest in. In these districts the Budgerigar forms great breeding-colonies. The "budgie" and the varieties that have been bred from it are among our most-loved bird pets.

FOOD: Millet and canary-grass seed.

BREEDING: These birds easily become tame and will incubate their eggs in a wooden box.

Budgerigar

POPULAR NAMES: **Red-backed Parakeet; Red-rumped Parakeet**

SCIENTIFIC NAME: *Psephotus haematonotus*

FAMILY: Psittacidae (Parrots)

SUB-FAMILY: Psittacinae (True Parrots)

Southeastern Australia is home to this 10½″-long (27 cm) bird which belongs to the long-tailed parakeet group. It lives in mallee scrub [grassland with scattered thickets formed by low-lying *Eucalyptus* shrubs] in flocks of all sizes, from small to large, and also visits town parks. Pairs keep together within the flock. The Red-backed Parakeet (its back is not visible in this photograph) has a strikingly attractive voice. It lives on seeds and green food and does not eat fruit. It nests in holes, the hen laying 4 to 7 eggs.

FOOD: Millet and canary-grass seeds, abundant greenstuff; also leaf-buds and grated carrots.

BREEDING: It is not uncommon for the Red-backed Parakeet to reproduce twice a year.

Red-backed Parakeet

Red-winged Parakeet; Crimson-winged Parakeet; Red-winged Lory

SCIENTIFIC NAME: *Aprosmictus erythropterus*
FAMILY: Psittacidae (Parrots)
SUB-FAMILY: Psittacinae (True Parrots)

Southern New Guinea and the north and north-east of Australia are the native territories of this bird, 13″ long (33 cm).

The Red-winged Parakeet lives in light forests, mostly in pairs or small flocks. It finds its food—fruit, flower nectar and insect larvae—chiefly in eucalyptus trees. Moreover, it prefers very deep tree holes as hatching-places. A clutch usually contains 2 to 4 eggs, which are incubated for 18 to 20 days.

FOOD: Similar to that usually given to parrots and parakeets. Supplement this with meal-worms and other insect larvae.

BREEDING: The Red-winged Parakeet will reproduce in captivity, although breeding these birds is a more difficult job than it is with the long-tailed parakeets described in the previous 10 pages.

Red-winged Parakeet

POPULAR NAME: **Ring-necked Parakeet**
SCIENTIFIC NAME: *Psittacula krameri*
FAMILY: Psittacidae (Parrots)
SUB-FAMILY: Psittacinae (True Parrots)

There are about 6 sub-species of this bird (about 16″ to 16½″ long; 40 to 42 cm long) living in western and northeastern Africa and in India, Ceylon, Burma, and southeastern China. It is a very popular household pet in many parts of its native territories. The Ring-necked Parakeet lives in thin forests, in farmland, and in the "gallery forests" lining the banks of rivers. It also makes its way into city parks. In its natural environment this bird feeds on a very wide variety of seeds and fruit. The Ring-necked Parakeet builds its nest in hollow trees and in holes in walls. It lays 3 to 5 eggs and incubates them for 24 days.

FOOD: The same as for the long-tailed parakeets.

BREEDING: The Ring-necked Parakeet can be successfully bred in captivity.

Ring-necked Parakeet

POPULAR NAME: **Masked Lovebird**
SCIENTIFIC NAME: *Agapornis personata personata*
FAMILY: Psittacidae (Parrots)
SUB-FAMILY: Psittacinae (True Parrots)

This $6\frac{1}{2}''$ (16 cm) bird is noted for its seemingly sociable nature. The Masked Lovebird lives in the light brushwood of Tanzania's seasonally arid savannas and feeds on various kinds of seeds and greenstuff. The Masked Lovebird forms small nesting-colonies, mostly in knot-holes and cracks of the baobab tree. It lays 3 to 6 eggs and incubates them for 23 days.

FOOD: Grain, foxtail-millet [Italian millet or *Setaria italica*], seeds, and greenstuff.

BREEDING: If kept in an aviary or a big cage, the Masked Lovebird will breed readily in a wooden nesting box, but it needs fresh twigs with which to build its nest.

Masked Lovebird

POPULAR NAME: **African Grey Parrot**
SCIENTIFIC NAME: *Psittacus erithacus*
FAMILY: Psittacidae (Parrots)
SUB-FAMILY: Psittacinae (True Parrots)

A member of the square-tailed parrot group and 14″ to 16″ (35 to 40 cm) long, this parrot comes in 3 sub-species. It is an inhabitant of western and central Africa's dense rain forests and mangrove woods. The African Grey Parrot lives in couples during the breeding season; at other times it forms big, noisy flocks. It lives on corn, nuts, bananas and other fruit and is therefore not welcome in plantations. As a nesting-place, it prefers a tree hole as high up as possible, where it lays 4 or 5 eggs.

FOOD: Seeds and corn; also swelled grain, nuts, young plant-shoots and plenty of fruit.

BREEDING: As popular as the African Grey Parrot is (it is the cleverest talker of all the parrots), it is unfortunately not easy to get this bird to breed in captivity.

African Grey Parrot

POPULAR NAME: **Senegal Parrot**
SCIENTIFIC NAME: *Poicephalus senegalus*
FAMILY: Psittacidae (Parrots)
SUB-FAMILY: Psittacinae (True Parrots)

Like the African Grey Parrot, this attractive bird is one of the square-tailed parrots; and the Senegal Parrot also exists in 3 sub-species. However, its natural haunts are the coastlands of western Africa. There, this $9\frac{1}{2}''$ long (24 cm) bird ranges the savannas with their scattered groups of trees and scrub, forming large flocks which, when the birds are hungry, can have devastating effects on fields and plantations. Normally, however, the Senegal Parrot stays high up in the trees, where it hatches its 2 or 3 eggs in natural holes. As a cage bird, it has proved to be an especially lovable and adaptable pet.

FOOD: The Senegal Parrot should be fed like the African Grey Parrot. Note though, that it is particularly fond of peanuts.

BREEDING: Unfortunately, attempts to make this parrot breed are rarely successful.

Senegal Parrot

POPULAR NAMES: **Black-headed Caique; Caique**
SCIENTIFIC NAME: *Pionites melanocephala*
FAMILY: Psittacidae (Parrots)
SUB-FAMILY: Psittacinae (True Parrots)

This 9½″ (24 cm) square-tailed parrot from Brazil is still a rather uncommon pet. As it lives chiefly on fruit, it is more difficult to feed than grain-eating parrots: it can be accustomed to grain-food, but only to a limited extent. The Black-headed Caique prefers to live in flocks in the gallery forests fringing riversides; it hatches its eggs in high-up tree holes.

FOOD: The Black-headed Caique's food is ripe bananas and other fruit, half-ripe corn cobs and greenstuff.

BREEDING: Successful breeding in captivity is exceptional.

Black-headed Caique

POPULAR NAMES: **Blue and Yellow Macaw; Yellow-breasted Macaw**

SCIENTIFIC NAME: *Ara ararauna*

FAMILY: Psittacidae (Parrots)

SUB-FAMILY: Psittacinae (True Parrots)

Averaging 37.2" (95 cm), this Macaw is the biggest of its genus. It lives in the jungles—from Panama to tropical-forest regions as far south as Bolivia and northern Paraguay. In its natural environment, the staple food of the Blue and Yellow Macaw is palm-fruit, which it breaks up effortlessly with its powerful beak. It also eats other tree-fruit and tree-shoots. The Blue and Yellow Macaw hatches its eggs in tree holes. After incubating their eggs, these birds form great flocks that may attack plantations. In captivity, there is no risk that a well-acclimatized Blue and Yellow Macaw will make any attempt to use its dangerous beak on its keeper. If you keep Macaws —or any other kind of parrot for that matter— remember that they are sociable creatures that like to have a lot of attention paid to them.

FOOD: In captivity, fruit, seeds, carrots, corn, nuts and lettuce.

BREEDING: In big aviaries the Blue and Yellow Macaw has been successfully bred many times.

Blue and Yellow Macaw

POPULAR NAME: **Celestial Parrotlet**
SCIENTIFIC NAME: *Forpus coelestis*
FAMILY: Psittacidae (Parrots)
SUB-FAMILY: Psittacinae (True Parrots)

This dwarf parrot [only 5″ (12 cm) long] belongs, like the big Macaws, to the genus of the wedge-tailed parakeets. It is found in 5 sub-species. The bird comes from Ecuador and Peru, where it lives sociably in thickets, in gallery forests, and in the sparsely wooded country of the drier districts. Its food consists mainly of tree-fruit and seeds. The Celestial Parrotlet hatches its eggs in tree holes. The incubation period is 17 days.

FOOD: In captivity, feed the Celestial Parrotlet with canary-grass seed, foxtail- [Italian-] or other millet seeds, oats and all kinds of greenstuff.

BREEDING: Until 1963, the Celestial Parrotlet did not breed in captivity, although it is sociable with other birds.

Celestial Parrotlet

POPULAR NAMES: **Grey-breasted Parakeet; Quaker Parakeet; Monk Parakeet**

SCIENTIFIC NAME: *Myiopsitta monachus*

FAMILY: Psittacidae (Parrots)

SUB-FAMILY: Psittacinae (True Parrots)

This South American wedge-tailed parakeet—10″ to 12″ long (26 to 30 cm)—is the only nest-building parrot. The nest is a "community" dwelling made of twigs high up in the trees, and several pairs of birds incubate their eggs in it. These nests are often as large as 3 feet in diameter (approximately 1 metre), and a tree may contain several of them. There are 4 to 6 eggs in every clutch. The Grey-breasted Parakeet lives in open woodland country, and big flocks of the birds often attack farmland.

FOOD: These birds live on fruit, seeds and greens.

BREEDING: A sociable bird, the Grey-breasted Parakeet is best kept in a large aviary, where it will breed.

NOTE: Recent reports indicate that the Grey-breasted or Quaker Parakeet may join pigeons and English sparrows as thriving non-native wild species in northern American cities. These birds either escaped from transporting crates or were released from their cages by negligent owners and have already proved their ability to survive the harsh winters of New York City and Nantucket

Grey-breasted Parakeet

Island and to reproduce and rear a generation of young there.

POPULAR NAMES: **Yellow-fronted Amazon; Surinam Amazon**
SCIENTIFIC NAME: *Amazona ochrocephala ochrocephala*
FAMILY: Psittacidae (Parrots)
SUB-FAMILY: Psittacinae (True Parrots)

The Amazons are among the tamest and most teachable of all parrots. Although sometimes called the "Surinam Amazon," the Yellow-fronted Amazon is to be found over great areas of South America and Trinidad. It is a popular pet both in its native territory and abroad.

Like all the Amazons, this 14½″ (37 cm) bird is a sociable jungle-dweller which also raids farms; it lives on fruit, seeds, and plant-shoots. The Yellow-fronted Amazon incubates its eggs in tree holes.

FOOD: In captivity, the same as the African Grey Parrot's.

BREEDING: It has not yet been possible to make this popular household pet breed in captivity.

Yellow-fronted Amazon

POPULAR NAME: **Violet-Ear**
SCIENTIFIC NAME: *Colibri coruscans*
FAMILY: Trochilidae (Hummingbirds)

This appealing bird has a wide distribution: from northern South America to northwest Argentina. The Violet-Ear lives in pairs in mountainous country and can also be seen in gardens of its native lands. Its nest is built near the ground on a thin limb, with 2 eggs being laid. Hummingbirds live on flower nectar, which they suck from the blossoms while hovering in the air. They also eat small insects. Slightly more than 4″ (11 cm) long, the Violet-Ear is one of the easiest hummingbirds to keep as a pet. It will quickly become tame, and you can let the Violet-Ears (and other hummingbird pets) fly about in the room and they will return to the cage. Most of them enjoy bathing.

FOOD: Caring for hummingbirds in captivity has become much simpler since it is now possible to make a nourishing liquid-food for them. You prepare this from a solution of sugar or honey in water, mixed with a protein-rich packaged product, and give it to the birds twice a day.

BREEDING: The Violet-Ear has been known to breed in captivity.

Violet-Ear

POPULAR NAME: **Red-tailed Amazilia**
SCIENTIFIC NAME: *Amazilia tzacatl*
FAMILY: Trochilidae (Hummingbirds)

Barely 4″ long (about 10 cm long), this Hummingbird lives in a territory extending from Mexico to Venezuela and Ecuador. It prefers tropical forests and their undergrowth and is fond of visiting plantations to gather nectar and small insects from flowers. It makes its nest in the brushwood or in forked boughs of trees. Males and females look very much alike.

FOOD: Feed the Red-tailed Amazilia just as you would the Violet-Ear.

BREEDING: The author does not know whether anyone has been successful in making the Red-tailed Amazilia breed in captivity, although it is fairly often on sale.

Red-tailed Amazilia

This tiny Sunbird—scarcely 4″ long (barely 10 cm)—exists in several sub-species, all of which live in southern, central and eastern Africa. The female is not so brightly colored as the male shown in the picture opposite. The Necklace Sunbird lives—in pairs or in small communities—in woods, parks, and plantations, where it prefers brushwood haunts. It subsists on flower nectar and small insects, thus helping to pollinate many plants—and in this respect the Sunbirds are like the hummingbirds. The hanging nest contains 2 or 3 eggs.

FOOD: Like the hummingbirds, the Necklace Sunbird can be fed with a packaged product rich in protein, dissolved in a solution of honey and water. It should also be given small insects.

Necklace Sunbird

POPULAR NAMES: **Emerald Toucanet; Crimson-
rumped Aracari**
SCIENTIFIC NAME: *Alaucorhynchus haematopygius*
FAMILY: Ramphastidae (Toucans)

This 16″ (40 cm) bird lives in the forests of the high
Colombian and Venezuelan Andes up to a height
of 10,000 feet (approximately 3,000 metres). Like
all of the toucans, the Emerald Toucanet prefers
to spend its time—in pairs or in small flocks—in the
tops of high trees and it is seldom to be seen on
the ground. It feeds on soft, juicy fruit, augmented
by insects, small reptiles and mammals and—
occasionally—by young birds. It makes its nest in
tree holes. The clutch of 2 to 4 eggs is incubated by
both the parents for 15 or 16 days. The fledglings
leave the nest 6 weeks after they have hatched.

Toucans enjoy flying, so the proper place for
them is a big aviary. They are rather quarrelsome
birds, toward their own species as well as with
outsiders.

FOOD: In captivity, the Emerald Toucanet and
its relations should be fed on dried and fresh fruit
of many kinds plus meal-worms and similar larvae.
Supplement this diet with boiled potatoes, carrots,
cooked rice and corn that you have formed into
small balls.

BREEDING: Unfortunately it has not yet been
possible to get this bird—or the other toucans—to
breed in captivity.

Emerald Toucanet

POPULAR NAMES: **Rainbow-billed Toucan; Fischer's Toucan; Sulphur-breasted Toucan; Keel-billed Toucan**

SCIENTIFIC NAME: *Ramphastus sulphuratus*

FAMILY: Ramphastidae (Toucans)

This bird is gifted with the most colorful beak of all the toucans. Hence its popular name. Averaging 18″ (45 cm), the bird comes from Guatemala, Honduras, and southeastern Mexico, where it lives in the tropical rain forests of the plains.

FOOD AND CARE: The comparatively peaceable Rainbow-billed Toucan needs the same kind of treatment as prescribed for the Emerald Toucanet (pages 72–73), but remember that as a decidedly tropical bird it has a great dislike for cold.

BREEDING: See Emerald Toucanet.

Rainbow-billed Toucan

POPULAR NAME: **Ariel Toucan**
SCIENTIFIC NAME: *Ramphastus ariel (R. vitellinus ariel)*
FAMILY: Ramphastidae (Toucans)

Approximately 18″ (45 cm) in length, this bird comes from the Amazon River area. Like the 2 other species of toucans described in pages 72–75, the Ariel Toucan is a tree-dweller that visits the ground only to bathe.

FOOD AND CARE: The Ariel Toucan soon becomes accustomed to captivity, but it feels really at home only in a very big aviary. This bird should be cared for in the same way as the Emerald Toucanet.

BREEDING: See Emerald Toucanet.

Ariel Toucan

POPULAR NAME: **Hoopoe**
SCIENTIFIC NAME: *Upupa epops*
FAMILY: Upupidae (Hoopoes)

Several sub-species of this 11″ to 12″ long (28 to 30 cm) bird live in open country in southern and central Europe and in Africa and Asia. While the Hoopoe is a very shy bird in Europe, in the East it is often to be found near human settlements. The Hoopoe lives chiefly on insects and their larvae. It nests in tree holes, cracks in walls and natural cavities or fissures in the ground. To protect herself from unwelcome visitors, the female bird secretes an extremely evil-smelling liquid. It quickly becomes tame in captivity.

FOOD: In captivity, meal-worms, earthworms, insects, meat, and the like.

BREEDING: A friendly bird, the Hoopoe may breed if kept in a spacious aviary.

Hoopoe

SCIENTIFIC NAME: *Pitta sordida cucullata*
FAMILY: Pittidae (Pittas)

This attractive $11\frac{1}{2}''$ (29 cm) bird is one of 15 sub-species of the Black-headed Pitta, which is distributed from India to Indo-China and Borneo, the Philippines and New Guinea. The bird originally came from India, where it still lives hidden in the jungle undergrowth. The Hooded Pitta finds its food—insects, spiders, worms and small reptiles—on the ground. It also eats berries and other kinds of fruit. The Hooded Pitta lays 2 to 6 eggs in a ball-shaped nest which it builds on the ground or near it, using grass, leaves and moss.

FOOD: Packaged soft food, fly-maggots, meal-worms, hard-boiled eggs, raw meat.

BREEDING: As a pet, this bird will thrive best in an aviary well-provided with growing plants and having a floor covered with earth and leaves. However, Pittas rarely breed in captivity.

Hooded Pitta

POPULAR NAME: **Bengal Pitta**
SCIENTIFIC NAME: *Pitta brachyura*
FAMILY: Pittidae (Pittas)

Several sub-species of this 7½″ (19 cm) Pitta live
in Indonesia, India, southeastern Asia, and Japan.
The Japanese sub-species spends the winter in
Taiwan. Like the Hooded Pitta, the Bengal Pitta
lives in the undergrowth and tree-roots of the
forests, where it scratches about in the leaves and
earth for insects, worms, and the like. It builds its
spherical nest on the ground. The eggs are incubated for 18 days, and the fledglings leave the
nest 16 days later.

FOOD: See Hooded Pitta, page 80.

BREEDING: Pittas rarely breed in captivity.

NOTE: Pittas from tropical Africa and America
are more rarely imported into Europe than the
Asian ones.

Bengal Pitta

POPULAR NAME: **Cotinga**
SCIENTIFIC NAME: *Cotinga amabilis*
FAMILY: Cotingidae (Cotingas)

Mexico and Central America are the native territory of this 8″ (20 cm) bird, an inhabitant of low-lying tropical forests. The Cotinga lives on fruit and insects. It makes a bowl-shaped nest, with the hen laying 2 to 4 eggs. The male (illustrated) is brightly colored, unlike the female.

FOOD: In captivity, fruit of almost any kind, rice that has been allowed to swell in water, finely chopped hard-boiled eggs, meal-worms, and insects. Remember that feeding the Cotinga—like catering for all fruit-eating birds—is a chore that cannot be neglected, for the bird must have fresh food twice a day.

BREEDING: No one has yet reported any success in getting this bird to breed in captivity.

Cotinga

POPULAR NAMES: **Andean Forest (Scarlet) Cock of the Rock; Peruvian Cock of the Rock**

SCIENTIFIC NAME: *Rupicola peruviana*

FAMILY: Cotingidae (Cotingas)

This Andean Forest species (approximately $12\frac{1}{2}''$— 32 cm) is less frequently seen in captivity than the Orange Cock of the Rock *(Rupicola rupicola)*. The Peruvian Cock of the Rock lives in humid tropical jungles, where it mostly stays on the ground, mating on rocks in surging rivers—thus its picturesque name. The mating display of this bird is quite famous: several males gather at the display ground and adopt static postures. They may hold these positions for minutes at a time.

In its natural environment the Peruvian Cock of the Rock lives on wild fruit, insects and reptiles and builds its bowl-shaped nest on rocky ground. As a rule, 2 eggs are laid.

FOOD: The Scarlet Cock of the Rock proves to be a sensitive bird in captivity and should be fed with fruit (it is very fond of grapes) as well as with cooked rice, carrots and insects.

Andean Forest (Scarlet) Cock of the Rock

POPULAR NAMES: **Green Bulbul; Hardwick's Fruit-
sucker; Orange-bellied Leafbird**
SCIENTIFIC NAME: *Chloropsis hardwickei*
FAMILY: Chloropseidae (Leafbirds)

This 8″ (20 cm) bird lives mostly in trees, where it
finds its food: fruit, insects and flower nectar. A
native of Burma, India and Thailand, the Green
Bulbul builds its nest, well-hidden from prying
eyes, high up in the trees. Its song is less beautiful
than that of the Golden-fronted Fruitsucker
(Chloropsis aurifrons, see pages 90–91); nevertheless,
the Green Bulbul's song contains some charming
phrases. Both of these fruit-eating birds make pets
that are easy to care for.

FOOD: See Blue-backed Fairy Bluebird, page 92.

BREEDING: So far it has not been possible to
breed the Green Bulbul in captivity, and it is not
offered for sale as often as the Golden-fronted
Fruitsucker.

Green   Bulbul

SCIENTIFIC NAME: *Chloropsis aurifrons*
FAMILY: Chloropseidae (Leafbirds)

Its attractive song makes this 11″ (28 cm) bird one of the most popular of the softbills and a much-sought-after pet. A friendly bird, even in a big aviary the Golden-browed Leafbird will soon eat from your hand. Its homeland extends from India to Sumatra; several sub-species live in this territory. Evergreen forests, its most preferred dwelling-place, provide the Golden-fronted Fruitsucker with food throughout the year: fruit, flower nectar and insects. The bird builds its nest in forked limbs, with the hen laying 2 or 3 eggs.

FOOD: In captivity also, its food should be varied, like that of the other Leafbirds.

BREEDING: Unfortunately the Golden-fronted Fruitsucker has not yet bred in captivity.

Golden-fronted Fruitsucker

POPULAR NAME: **Blue-backed Fairy Bluebird**
SCIENTIFIC NAME: *Irena puella*
FAMILY: Chloropseidae (Leafbirds)

Some zoologists include this $9\frac{1}{2}''$ (24 cm) bird in
the Oriole family. It comes from India and Indo-
China, where it lives in the tropical rain forests,
either in pairs (during the incubating season) or
in small flocks. The Blue-backed Fairy Bluebird
lives on soft, juicy wild fruit, but varies this diet
with insects and flower nectar—and in this way it
helps to pollinate several kinds of coral trees
(Erythrina). The plainly colored female builds her
bowl-shaped nest in shady spots at a height of
5 to 20 feet ($1\frac{1}{2}$ to 6 metres).

FOOD: Fruit such as dates, grapes, pears, and
apples—chopped up small—as well as hard-
boiled eggs and raw meat, should supplement a
universal packaged food.

BREEDING: The Blue-backed Fairy Bluebird will
be most likely to breed in an aviary supplied with
plenty of greenery.

Blue-backed Fairy Bluebird

POPULAR NAME: **Red-eared Bulbul**
SCIENTIFIC NAME: *Pycnonotus jocosus emeria*
FAMILY: Pycnonotidae (Bulbuls)

In a distribution area extending from India to Malaysia and China, several quite varied sub-species of this bird thrive. [8″ (20 cm) is the most frequently encountered length.] The Red-eared Bulbul feeds on ripe and unripe fruit and on insects. It is a gentle, sociable bird that lives in the borders of forests or in parks and gardens. Never-theless, the Red-eared Bulbul can do quite a lot of damage in orchards. The bird builds its nest in dense undergrowth, the hen laying 2, 3 or 4 eggs. The Red-eared Bulbul quickly becomes tame in captivity. It sings nicely and has a wide repertoire of melodies.

FOOD: In captivity, a packaged soft food, fruit, insects and seeds.

BREEDING: It has sometimes been successfully bred in captivity.

Red-eared Bulbul

POPULAR NAMES: **Golden-eyed Babbler; Babbling Thrush**

SCIENTIFIC NAME: *Chrysomma sinenese*
FAMILY: Muscicapidae (Old World Flycatchers)
SUB-FAMILY: Timaliinae (Babblers)

India, Burma, Thailand, Laos, and China are home territory to this appealing bird. Averaging 7" (17½ cm), the Golden-eyed Babbler comes in several sub-species. It is a bird of the open grasslands, bushlands, open high-lying forests, and gardens and parks. In all these places it feeds on insects and fruit—either in pairs or in small flocks of 8 to 12 birds. The Golden-eyed Babbler builds its nest in forked limbs. It is a lively but friendly bird, well-suited for living in a community aviary.

FOOD: Packaged insectivorous food, juicy fruit, egg-food, meal-worms and other larvae, and insects.

Golden-eyed Babbler

POPULAR NAME: **Peking Nightingale**
SCIENTIFIC NAME: *Leiothrix lutea*
FAMILY: Muscicapidae (Old World Flycatchers)
SUB-FAMILY: Timaliinae (Babblers)

One of the best-known of all the Babblers, this 5″ (13 cm) Asiatic bird comes in 6 sub-species. The undergrowth of the oak and coniferous forests in the mountainous regions of India, Sikkim, Burma, and China are its natural haunts. The Peking Nightingale lives on insects, worms and small seeds as well as on berries and other wild fruits. Its sonorous song makes the bird particularly popular. During the breeding season, the Peking Nightingale lays 3 or 4 eggs.

If you keep a Peking Nightingale (or more than one) in a cage, let it (or them) out as often as possible to fly about in the room.

FOOD: In captivity a universal cage-bird food, millet and canary seeds, greenstuff—and at least 10 meal-worms per bird per day.

BREEDING: Among amateur bird-keepers, only those with experience are generally successful in getting the Peking Nightingale to breed in captivity. You should know, too, that in an aviary with plenty of greenery, the bird is likely to disturb other nesting birds.

Peking Nightingale

POPULAR NAMES: **Black-chinned Flowerpecker;**
Yuhina

SCIENTIFIC NAME: *Yuhina nigrimenta*
FAMILY: Muscicapidae (Old World Flycatchers)
SUB-FAMILY: Timaliinae (Babblers)

Only 4″ (10 cm) long, this Babbler is a dainty, lively bird from India and Indo-China. It lives sociably in highland bushwoods and is constantly on the move, looking for insects. Soft fruit augments its diet. The Black-chinned Flowerpecker lays 3 eggs; the young birds leave the eggs 12 days after the start of incubation and quit the nest 2 weeks later.

FOOD AND CARE: In captivity, feed the Black-chinned Flowerpecker with packaged, universal softbill food and with fruit flies, ants' eggs, mealworms, fruit, and honey-water. Because it is a sociable bird, at least a pair of these birds should be kept in the aviary.

BREEDING: These birds sometimes breed successfully in captivity.

Black-chinned Flowerpecker

POPULAR NAMES: **Himalayan Mountain Robin; Blue-headed Rock Thrush**

SCIENTIFIC NAME: *Monticola cinclorhynchus*

FAMILY: Muscicapidae (Old World Flycatchers)

SUB-FAMILY: Turdinae (Thrushes)

The thin forests of the Himalayas, growing at altitudes of 5,000 to 10,000 feet (1,500 to 3,500 metres), play host to this 7″ (11 cm) bird. However, the Himalayan Mountain Robin spends the winter farther south: in India, Burma, and Thailand. The Himalayan Mountain Robin's food consists of insects, small batrachians (froglike and toadlike animals), and reptiles. The female is more plainly colored than the male bird shown in this picture. The Himalayan Mountain Robin builds its nest in holes or hollows in rocks, or among tangled roots that have attached themselves to rocks. There are 3, 4 or 5 eggs, which the young birds leave after 17 days. The male bird sings busily while the eggs are being hatched.

FOOD: Feed this bird with soft food and with insects, meal-worms and the like.

BREEDING: The Himalayan Mountain Robin has been known to breed in captivity.

Himalayan Mountain Robin

POPULAR NAME: **Shama**
SCIENTIFIC NAME: *Copsychus malabaricus*
FAMILY: Muscicapidae (Old World Flycatchers)
SUB-FAMILY: Turdinae (Thrushes)

A good mimic, this bird is moreover the best and most creatively musical of all exotic songbirds. The 17 sub-species of the Shama inhabit a territory extending from India to Indo-China and Indonesia. The birds live there singly or in pairs in the bamboo forests fringing the rivers. Averaging a length of $9\frac{1}{2}''$ (24 cm) (including its tail) the Shama hunts insects of all kinds and also eats wild fruit. It makes its bowl-shaped nest in tree holes. The Shama quickly becomes tame, but is unfortunately inclined to be quarrelsome, both with birds of its own species and with other small birds.

FOOD: Universal food for cage birds, supplemented with ants' eggs, meal-worms, shredded meat, hard-boiled eggs, raisins, fresh fruit, and the like.

BREEDING: Prospects for success will be best if the bird is kept in an aviary well-provided with green vegetation.

Shama

POPULAR NAMES: **Dama Thrush; Orange-headed Ground Thrush**

SCIENTIFIC NAME: *Zoothera citrina*

FAMILY: Muscicapidae (Old World Flycatchers)

SUB-FAMILY: Turdinae (Thrushes)

The dense mountain forests of India, Burma, Thailand, and southern China are the home of this 8″ (20 to 21 cm) bird that will live at altitudes of up to about 4,000 feet (1,200 metres). The Dama Thrush does not have the lively temperament of the Shama and often stays out of sight in the undergrowth of its high-elevation haunts.

The Dama lives mainly on insects and their larvae, berries, and other ripe fruit. It makes its nest in forked limbs that are 3 to 6 or 7 feet above the ground (1 to approximately 2 metres above ground-level). The male has a very attractive song.

FOOD: In addition to universal cage-bird food, give the Dama shredded carrots, meal-worms, raw beef, curds, soft fruit, and all kinds of greenstuff.

Dama Thrush

POPULAR NAME: **Rufous-bellied Niltava**
SCIENTIFIC NAME: *Niltava sundara*
FAMILY: Muscicapidae (Old World Flycatchers)
SUB-FAMILY: Muscicapinae (True Flycatchers)

Between 6″ and 6½″ long (16 to 17 cm), this bird lives on the wooded slopes of the Himalayas at heights of 5,000 to 8,000 feet (1,500 to 2,500 metres). Partial to dense undergrowth, it hunts insects near the ground and also eats fruit. The Niltava often builds its nest near water, which it likes to have nearby. The nest contains 3 or 4 eggs, which are incubated for 14 days. The young birds leave the nest 10 to 12 days later.

FOOD: The Niltava should be fed just like the thrushes (pages 102–107).

BREEDING: Successful breeding of these birds in captivity is exceptional; the most beneficial environment is a big aviary with lots of greenery. The mother bird will be able to find there the insects she needs for her well-being.

Rufous-bellied Niltava

POPULAR NAME: **Indian White-eye**
SCIENTIFIC NAME: *Zosterops palpebrosa*
FAMILY: Zosteropidae (White-eyes)

This petite (4″; 10 cm) bird is at home in India and Ceylon. Living at heights of up to about 5,600 feet (1,700 metres), the Indian White-eye inhabits woods, bushes, gardens and parks. A charming and peaceable bird, the Indian White-eye also has a melodious song that makes it very popular. It lives on insects, flower nectar and all kinds of fruit. The hanging, bowl-shaped nest is built in bushes between two branches. The hen lays 2 or 3 eggs.

FOOD: In captivity, the Indian White-eye should be given universal cage-bird food, honey-water, insects—including meal-worms and fruit flies—and soft fruit.

BREEDING: These birds have been known to breed if there is a secluded corner of the cage or aviary.

Indian White-eye

POPULAR NAME: **Japanese Waxwing**
SCIENTIFIC NAME: *Bombycilla japonica*
FAMILY: Bombycillidae (Waxwings)

Barely 8″ (20 cm) long, this bird nests in eastern Siberia and Manchuria and, despite its name, visits Japan only as a winter guest. It differs from the native Bohemian Waxwing *(Bombycilla garrulus)* by having a red tail: the native species has a yellow one. The Japanese Waxwing inhabits the northern birchwoods and forests of coniferous trees, living on seeds, berries and insects. It catches midges while in flight. Its nest, built in a treetop, contains 4 to 7 eggs, which are incubated for 14 days.

FOOD: In captivity, the Japanese Waxwing should be fed with universal cage-bird food, ants' eggs, apples and berries.

NOTE: The Bohemian Waxwing or *Bombycilla garrulus* is sometimes also called the European Waxwing. It is a native American species and holarctic as well (that is, native to Europe, Asia and America in the northern hemisphere). In America this yellow-tailed Waxwing is protected by law so that it is illegal to catch or keep any of them. In Europe, however, it is permissible to keep the Bohemian Waxwing and this bird is, in fact, more often kept in a cage than is the Japanese Waxwing. Feed the Bohemian (or European)

Japanese Waxwing

Waxwing the same food as you would the Japanese Waxwing.

POPULAR NAME: **Red-crested Finch**
SCIENTIFIC NAME: *Coryphospingus cucullatus*
FAMILY: Emberizidae (Buntings)
SUB-FAMILY: Emberizinae (True Buntings)

The male bird (illustrated) has a crest, which it raises a little only when it is singing. About 5½″ (14 cm) long, the Red-crested Finch lives in Brazil, the Guianas, northern Argentina, and Bolivia, preferring open country with scattered bushes and groups of trees. It hunts for seeds and insects in the dense undergrowth and grass. The Red-crested Finch makes its nest in bushes, the hen laying 3 or 4 eggs. It is often difficult to acclimatize newly imported birds to captivity.

FOOD: Besides the usual grain, this bird needs an assortment of greenstuff as well as ants' eggs and living insects. Young birds, however, are fed almost entirely on insects.

BREEDING: Red-crested Finches have sometimes bred in captivity.

Red-crested Finch

POPULAR NAMES: **Purple-crowned Finch; Ecuadorian Crowned Finch**

SCIENTIFIC NAME: *Rhodospingus cruentus*

FAMILY: Emberizidae (Buntings)

SUB-FAMILY: Emberizinae (True Buntings)

A very well-hidden existence in light-forest or high-lying brushwood is the life-style of this $4\frac{1}{2}''$ (11 cm) bird. Ecuador and Peru are its native territory. The Purple-crowned Finch (also often called the Ecuadorian Crowned Finch) feeds on various kinds of seeds and insects. It lays 3 eggs, which are incubated for 11 or 12 days. The fledglings leave the nest 12 days later.

FOOD: Feed the Purple-crowned Finch with grain, greenstuff, meal-worms, and ants' eggs.

BREEDING: In captivity, Purple-crowned Finches have repeatedly bred in a small basket, a canary's cage, or the abandoned nest of a weaverbird; this Finch has also been known to build a free-standing nest of its own out of bast (woody fibre from plants, shrubs and trees of the linden family) and coconut fibre. Unfortunately though, this good-natured bird is seldom on sale.

Purple-crowned Finch

POPULAR NAME: **Lesser Cuba Finch**
SCIENTIFIC NAME: *Tiaris canora*
FAMILY: Emberizidae (Buntings)
SUB-FAMILY: Emberizinae (True Buntings)

Unlike the Greater Cuba Finch, or Olive Finch *(Tiaris olivacea)*, this diminutive bird (4"; 9½ to 10 cm) is found only in Cuba. It lives in pairs in the plentiful bushes of that island's grassy plains. The Lesser Cuba Finch feeds on seeds of many kinds and on small insects. This little bird builds its spherical nest high up in the trees. It lays 2, 3 or 4 eggs, which the young birds leave after 12 days; 15 days later they fly away from the nest. Meanwhile, during the nesting season, the male bird is very aggressive toward other birds.

FOOD: Canary-grass seed, millet, foxtail millet, greenstuff, unripe grass seed, soft food, insects and ants' eggs. The young birds should be fed with living insects only.

BREEDING: The Lesser Cuba Finch quickly becomes tame and will breed even in a cage.

Lesser Cuba Finch

POPULAR NAME: **Black-crested Finch**
SCIENTIFIC NAME: *Lophospingus pussilus*
FAMILY: Emberizidae (Buntings)
SUB-FAMILY: Emberizinae (True Buntings)

Southern Bolivia, western Argentina, and Paraguay are the home territory of this $4\frac{1}{2}$″ long bird (12 cm). The Black-crested Finch lives in parklike country endowed with scattered bushwood and lives on seeds and insects. It builds a bowl-shaped nest where 2 or 3 eggs are laid. The young birds leave the eggs after 14 days and can fly 3 weeks later. The Black-crested Finch is a lively but friendly bird.

FOOD: In captivity, feed the Black-crested Finch grain, including foxtail millet and unripe grass seed, plus greenstuff, ants' eggs, meal-worms, and living insects.

BREEDING: The Black-crested Finch often breeds in captivity.

Black-crested Finch

POPULAR NAMES: **Cardinal; Pyrrhuloxia**
SCIENTIFIC NAME: *Pyrrhuloxia cardinalis*
FAMILY: Emberizidae (Buntings)
SUB-FAMILY: Pyrrhuloxiinae (Cardinals)

The distribution area of this 8″ or 8½″ bird (approximately 21 or 22 cm) extends from eastern North America to Mexico and British Honduras. Mostly in pairs, the bird inhabits small woods and bushwoods and appears also in gardens and parks, where it hunts for insects, insect larvae, seeds, berries and flowers. This Cardinal is a good songster.

FOOD: Mixed grain, sunflower seeds, peanuts, chopped fruit, greenstuff, corn and living insects.

BREEDING: It has often been possible to breed the Cardinal successfully in a well-planted aviary.

Cardinal

POPULAR NAME: **Green Cardinal**
SCIENTIFIC NAME: *Gubernatrix cristata*
FAMILY: Emberizidae (Buntings)
SUB-FAMILY: Pyrrhuloxiinae (Cardinals)

This attractive 7″ long (approximately 17½ cm) bird is at home in Argentina. The Green Cardinal prefers open country with plenty of dense groups of bushes, where it searches for seeds, insects, and worms on the ground or in the brushwood. The bowl-shaped nest is built, well-hidden from view, in dense brush near the ground. The Green Cardinal's 2 or 3 eggs are incubated by both parents.

FOOD: It should be given the same kind of food as the Cardinal, pages 122–123. Increase the proportion of egg-food and living insects while the birds are incubating.

BREEDING: Like many other birds, this Cardinal is quarrelsome during its breeding time, but that will have no serious consequences if you keep the bird in a big aviary.

Buntings

Green Cardinal

POPULAR NAMES: **Grey Cardinal; Red-crested Cardinal**

SCIENTIFIC NAME: *Paroaria coronata*
FAMILY: Emberizidae (Buntings)
SUB-FAMILY: Pyrrhuloxiinae (Cardinals)

About 7½″ (19 cm) long, this Cardinal is at home in southern Brazil and in Bolivia and Argentina. Like the other cardinals in this book, it inhabits fairly open country interspersed with scattered groups of bushes and trees; it is fond of places near rivers and also occasionally visits villages and towns. The Grey Cardinal lives on seeds, insects, worms and fruit. The bird builds its nest in dense undergrowth. The 3 to 4 eggs are incubated for 14 days, and the fledglings leave the nest 2 weeks later.

FOOD: The Grey Cardinal needs the same kinds of food as the Green Cardinal.

BREEDING: In captivity, the Grey Cardinal will accept a small basket or a nesting box as a foundation for the nest.

Grey Cardinal

POPULAR NAME: **Indigo Bunting**
SCIENTIFIC NAME: *Passerina cyanea*
FAMILY: Emberizidae (Buntings)
SUB-FAMILY: Pyrrhuloxiinae (Cardinals)

This aptly named bird nests in Canada and the United States and spends the winter in Mexico, Central America, the Bahamas and Cuba. The Indigo Bunting, averaging 5″ (12½ cm), leads quite a secluded life in the brushwood of forest borders and parks and gardens, where it gathers seeds, flower buds, leaf-shoots and berries. It builds its nest in dense undergrowth. The eggs—4 or 5—are incubated by the female for 13 days. The young birds leave the nest 12 days later. In the winter the male loses his magnificent plumage, so that at this time of the year he can hardly be distinguished from the female.

FOOD: In captivity, the Indigo Bunting should be fed with universal packaged cage-bird food, millet, niger seed (ramtil seed), canary-grass seed, maw (a kind of poppy seed), rape seed, hemp seed, egg-food, white bread softened in milk, meal-worms, ants' eggs, greenstuff, and fruit chopped small.

BREEDING: The Indigo Bunting is most likely to breed in an aviary containing plenty of vegetation.

Indigo Bunting

POPULAR NAME: **Rainbow Bunting**
SCIENTIFIC NAME: *Passerina leclancheri*
FAMILY: Emberizidae (Buntings)
SUB-FAMILY: Pyrrhuloxiinae (Cardinals)

The dense lowland forests of southwestern Mexico
are the home of this 5″ (13 cm) bird. The Rainbow
Bunting spends most of its time in the underbrush
and on the ground, feeding on seeds, insects,
greenstuff and fruit. The nest, usually concealed
in dense undergrowth, contains 2 or 3 eggs. The
song of the male bird is low but pleasing. Unfortunately the Rainbow Bunting is quite a
delicate bird, needing much warmth; and par-
ticular care must be taken to try to make it feel at
home in captivity. The proper place for this shy
bird is an aviary containing plenty of greenery
and heated in the winter.

FOOD: The Rainbow Bunting needs a varied
diet: in addition to grain, give it unripe grass
seed, greenstuff, soft food, living insects, and
spiders.

Rainbow Bunting

POPULAR NAMES: **Painted Bunting; Nonpareil**
SCIENTIFIC NAME: *Passerina ciris*
FAMILY: Emberizidae (Buntings)
SUB-FAMILY: Pyrrhuloxiinae (Cardinals)

Another 5″ (13 cm) Bunting: but this one nests in the southern and southeastern areas of the United States and spends the winter in Mexico, Panama, Cuba, and the Bahamas. It prefers bushes and forest borders and is fond of orchards. The Painted Bunting makes its nest in dense thickets. It lays 3 or 4 eggs which are incubated by the female alone for 13 days. The young birds leave the nest 12 days afterwards.

FOOD: Give this bird the same kind of food as you would the Indigo Bunting.

BREEDING: In an aviary well-supplied with vegetation, the Painted Bunting will breed.

Painted Bunting

POPULAR NAME: **Golden-eared Tanager**
SCIENTIFIC NAME: *Tangara chrysotis*
FAMILY: Emberizidae (Buntings)
SUB-FAMILY: Thraupinae (Tanagers)

Colombia, eastern Ecuador, Peru and northern Bolivia are the native territories of this attractive $5\frac{1}{2}''$ (14 cm) Tanager. Because it lives in the thickly forested lower slopes of the Andes (in all the above countries), this bird manages to remain well camouflaged despite its iridescent plumage. Insects, insect larvae and fruit form this bird's principal diet. The Golden-eared Tanager lays 2 or 3 eggs. It is rarely imported, and when it is, needs careful acclimatization. Once it has been made to feel at home in an aviary, it will prove to be—like many of its relations—a contented bird. However, more time must be spent looking after the Golden-eared Tanager (as is the case with all of the fruit-eating birds) than is needed for seed-eaters.

FOOD: Ripe fruit, packaged soft food, ants' eggs and living insects.

Golden-eared Tanager

POPULAR NAME: **Paradise Tanager**
SCIENTIFIC NAME: *Tangara chilensis*
FAMILY: Emberizidae (Buntings)
SUB-FAMILY: Thraupinae (Tanagers)

There are 3 sub-species of this $5\frac{1}{2}''$ to $6''$ Tanager (approximately $14\frac{1}{2}$ cm) living in a territory covering Colombia, Ecuador, Bolivia, Peru, the Guianas and Brazil. The bird does not dwell in Chile, even though its zoological name means "Chilean Tanager." It lives in the dense tropical forests east of the Andes. This insect- and fruit-eating Tanager builds its well-camouflaged nests in trees.

FOOD: The Paradise Tanager should be given the same kind of food as the Golden-eared Tanager.

BREEDING: As naturalists have been able to make only very few scientific observations of this bird in its native territory, it would be very interesting if the Paradise Tanager could be bred in captivity. But as far as the author is aware, it has not yet done so.

Paradise Tanager

POPULAR NAME: **Blue-headed Tanager**
SCIENTIFIC NAME: *Tangara cyanicollis*
FAMILY: Emberizidae (Buntings)
SUB-FAMILY: Thraupinae (Tanagers)

One of our most popular tanagers, this 5½" (13½ to 14 cm) bird comes from northwestern Venezuela and from Ecuador, Colombia, Brazil, Peru and Bolivia. In all these countries it lives in the open tropical forests and—at greater heights above sea level—in the subtropical forests. Its natural diet consists of many different kinds of fruit, insects, and spiders. The Blue-headed Tanager's open, bowl-shaped nest is built, well-concealed, in trees. As a rule, the nest contains 2 eggs.

FOOD: The Blue-headed Tanager needs the same kind of care, food and treatment as the other Tanagers.

BREEDING: In captivity, this Tanager has been bred by experienced bird-fanciers.

Blue-headed Tanager

POPULAR NAME: **Superb Tanager**
SCIENTIFIC NAME: *Tangara fastuosa*
FAMILY: Emberizidae (Buntings)
SUB-FAMILY: Thraupinae (Tanagers)

This 5½″ (13½ to 14 cm) Tanager is native to the eastern parts of Brazil. It lives in pairs, or in small flocks, high up in the trees of the rain forests. There it can find enough of its staple foods: fruit and insects. But the Superb Tanager also visits gardens and plantations and shows little fear of people. Like all the tanagers, it is fond of bathing. This bird builds its nest in dense undergrowth.

FOOD AND CARE: This bird thrives best if it is given the same kind of food as the other tanagers (pages 134–139) and if it is given a large aviary where there is ample scope for its lively temperament to develop properly. Like most of the tanagers, the Superb Tanager needs warmth.

Superb Tanager

POPULAR NAME: **Golden-green Tanager**
SCIENTIFIC NAME: *Tangara schrankii*
FAMILY: Emberizidae (Buntings)
SUB-FAMILY: Thraupinae (Tanagers)

Several sub-species of this 5″ (12 to 13 cm) Tanager live in the evergreen tropical forests of southern Venezuela, eastern Ecuador and northern Bolivia, as well as in Brazil and Peru east of the Andes. The Golden-green Tanager is a lively bird, found in pairs or in small flocks—and thanks to its green color it is well camouflaged in its native territory. It feeds on insects, small spiders and wild fruit.

FOOD AND CARE: It should be tended and fed in captivity in the same way as you would care for other iridescent tanagers of the *Tangara* genus (pages 134–141).

Golden-green Tanager

POPULAR NAMES: **Violet-blue Euphonia; Violet Tanager**

SCIENTIFIC NAME: *Tanagra violacea*

FAMILY: Emberizidae (Buntings)

SUB-FAMILY: Thraupinae (Tanagers)

This $3\frac{1}{2}''$ to $4''$ bird (approximately 9–10 cm) is at home in northern South America and in Trinidad. It lives in light forests and in scrub, feeding mainly on fruit and insects. The Violet-blue Euphonia builds its nest in well-hidden spots in dense brushwood: the hen lays 3 or 4 eggs which are incubated for 13 or 14 days. The fledglings leave the nest 3 weeks later.

After nesting-time, the Violet-blue Euphonia attacks orchards in great flocks and does a lot of damage in its native lands.

FOOD: Feed it with ripe fruit, living insects and packaged soft food.

BREEDING: In captivity, the Violet-blue Euphonia has been known to breed in small nesting boxes.

Violet-blue Euphonia

POPULAR NAME: **Scarlet Tanager**
SCIENTIFIC NAME: *Ramphocelus bresilius*
FAMILY: Emberizidae (Buntings)
SUB-FAMILY Thraupinae (Tanagers)

At 7″ (18 cm), this bird is one of the commonest tanagers of eastern Brazil. Only the male (illustrated) shows the typical brilliant red color: the much less noticeable female is brownish. The Scarlet Tanager lives—in small flocks—in the grasslands with their scattered bushwoods and reedy swamps. The bird builds its nest in dense undergrowth, the hen laying 2 or 3 eggs. The Scarlet Tanager lives on berries, insects, and worms. It is imported in large numbers and is a resistant bird although it is reputed to be unsociable and to be a nest-robber if it has a chance.

FOOD: The Scarlet Tanager should be fed like the other tanagers.

BREEDING: These birds are known to breed in captivity.

Scarlet Tanager

SCIENTIFIC NAME: *Amblyrhamphus holosericeus*
FAMILY: Icteridae (Icterids)

This 9½″ (24 cm) bird comes from Argentina and Paraguay, where it lives in swampland and marshy areas abounding in reeds and rushes. It also visits agricultural land, and great flocks often call at fields of corn. However, the Red-headed Marshbird does not live entirely on seeds. It has just as much appetite for insects, worms and fruit. The bird builds its nest in reeds. Its song contains melodious phrases, but also some harsh themes. In captivity, the Red-headed Marshbird may be dangerous to smaller birds if it has to share living-space with them. Fresh willow twigs will make it happy, for it can sharpen its beak on them.

FOOD: In captivity, the Red-headed Marshbird should be fed with thrush food, insects, peeled oats, corn, rice, millet seed and fruit.

Red-headed Marshbird

POPULAR NAME: **Siskin**
SCIENTIFIC NAME: *Carduelis spinus*
FAMILY: Fringillidae (Finches)

This inhabitant of northern, central and eastern Europe is one of the most popular of all cage birds. During the breeding season it keeps to coniferous forests, where it usually builds its well-camouflaged nest high up in the trees. The hen lays 4 to 6 eggs which she incubates alone, for 11 to 14 days. The young birds leave the nest 13 to 15 days later. Adults average $4\frac{1}{2}''$ to 5" (12 cm).

Outside the incubation period, the Siskin can be seen in water-meadow coppices, by the shores of lakes and rivers and in parks and gardens. It lives on tree seeds and other seeds and on buds and small insects. The Siskin quickly becomes tame.

FOOD: As varied as possible—grain, greenstuff, ants' eggs, meal-worms, and aphids.

BREEDING: The Siskin is most likely to breed if kept in an aviary, but the young birds will not survive unless they can be given their fill of insects.

Siskin

Guatemala, Nicaragua and southeastern Mexico are home to this species of Siskin, again about $4\frac{1}{2}''$ or $5''$ (12 cm) long. In these countries the Black-breasted Siskin lives in fairly high-lying forests of coniferous trees and oaks. The male bird can be distinguished by its pleasant song. The Black-breasted Siskin lives on many kinds of seeds and small insects. It builds its nest in high trees, the hen laying 3 to 4 eggs. After nesting, the bird forms small flocks.

FOOD: In captivity this bird should be given the same kind of food as the European Goldfinch.

Black-breasted Siskin

POPULAR NAME: **Bullfinch**
SCIENTIFIC NAME: *Pyrrhula pyrrhula*
FAMILY: Fringillidae (Finches)

This attractive bird—about 6″ (15 cm) long—lives in pairs in European forests of coniferous and mixed trees—also in parks and cemeteries. Wintertime, it can be seen flying in small flocks. The Bullfinch makes its nest in coniferous trees, the hen laying 3 to 5 eggs; these are incubated by the female, who is less colorful than her mate. The young birds leave the eggs after 13 or 14 days and fly out 16 to 18 days later. The Bullfinch lives on seeds of many kinds and on berries, flower buds, small insects, and spiders. It quickly becomes tame in captivity.

FOOD: Hemp seed, sunflower seeds, cheese, berries, greens and half-ripe seeds.

BREEDING: The Bullfinch is most likely to breed in an aviary with plenty of vegetation.

Bullfinch

POPULAR NAME: **European Goldfinch**
SCIENTIFIC NAME: *Carduelis carduelis*
FAMILY: Fringillidae (Finches)

Not only does it have an attractive song, but this $4\frac{1}{2}''$ to $5''$ (approximately 12 cm) Goldfinch is also one of the most colorful of all European birds. It inhabits the whole of that continent except the far north, with its distribution area extending to northern Africa and Asia and as far east as India and central Asia. It is not native to the United States, but has been introduced into America and now breeds on Long Island.

The European Goldfinch likes open country with undergrowth and patches of woodland, as well as open mixed forests; it also visits gardens. This bird makes its nest in the forked limbs of trees, the hen laying 3 to 6 eggs which are incubated for 12 to 14 days. The European Goldfinch lives on seeds although it feeds its young mostly with insects.

FOOD: Semi-ripe and ripe seeds, greenstuff, insects.

BREEDING: The European Goldfinch will breed in an aviary.

European Goldfinch

POPULAR NAME: **Canary**
SCIENTIFIC NAME: *Serinus canaria domesticus*
FAMILY: Fringillidae (Finches)

Over the years an abundance of different kinds of canaries, widely varying in shape, color and song, have been bred from this bird. Originally a quite ordinary-looking yellow-green bird, the Canary is native to the Canary Islands, Madeira, and the Azores. Canaries with red plumage derive from cross-breeding with the scarlet South American Hooded Siskin *(Spinus cucullatus)*. The improved varieties of the Canary are more resistant and easier to breed than the original bird.

FOOD: All canaries should be fed with mixed grain consisting of rape seed, foxtail (Italian) and ordinary millet, canary-grass seed, maw and niger seed (see page 128) and hemp, augmented with soft food, green plants, and some fruit. Additional egg-food and biscuits should be added for bringing up the young birds.

BREEDING: The bird (it lays 4 or 5 eggs) will readily breed in canary-cages.

Canary

POPULAR NAMES: **Yellow-fronted Canary; Green Singing Finch; Mozambique Serin**

SCIENTIFIC NAME: *Serinus mozambicus*

FAMILY: Fringillidae (Finches)

Several sub-species of this $4\frac{1}{2}''$ (11 cm) bird live in southeastern and eastern Africa as far west as the Congo and up the continent to Ethiopia. In its native territory the bird frequents open groups of trees and undergrowth in the savannas, as well as farmland and gardens. The Yellow-fronted Canary prefers to look for its food—seeds and green plant-shoots—on the ground. It builds its nest in bushes or in forked limbs of trees. The nest contains 3 or 4 eggs; the young birds leave the eggs after 13 days and fly off 3 weeks later. Because of its melodious song, the Yellow-fronted Canary is a treasured cage and aviary bird.

FOOD AND CARE: It needs the same kind of care and food as the Canary. At breeding time it should be given additional insects, ants' eggs, and egg-food.

BREEDING: This bird will breed in captivity, but supply the pair with baskets or nest boxes.

Yellow-fronted Canary

POPULAR NAME: **Sudan Golden Sparrow**
SCIENTIFIC NAME: *Passer luteus luteus*
FAMILY: Ploceidae (Weaverbirds)
SUB-FAMILY: Passerinae (Sparrows)

This 5″ (13 cm) Sparrow often appears in its native territory—the Sudan, the Sahara Desert, and northern Nigeria—in great swarms. It lives in dry grasslands, but often also visits farms, towns, and villages. The Sudan Golden Sparrow feeds on grass seed and insects. It builds its nest in trees or scrub, forming nesting-colonies. The hen lays 3 or 4 eggs which are incubated for 10 to 12 days. In captivity, the bird is lively, but friendly, if kept in an aviary.

FOOD: The Sudan Golden Sparrow should be given the usual grain mixture fed to the weaver-finches—that is, foxtail millet plus soft food, greenstuff and meal-worms.

Sudan Golden Sparrow

POPULAR NAME: **Senegal Combassou**
SCIENTIFIC NAME: *Hypochera chalybeata*
FAMILY: Ploceidae (Weaverbirds)
SUB-FAMILY: Viduinae (Whydahs)

Several sub-species of this $4\frac{1}{2}''$ (11 cm) bird live in Africa's dry grasslands, from the Sudan west to Senegambia [the area of the Senegal and Gambia Rivers]. The Senegal Combassous dwell mostly in the savanna and in fields, where they can find seeds as well as insects. Outside the incubation period, the male has inconspicuous greyish-brown plumage. The Senegal Combassou does not build a nest: like all the whydahs it is a nest parasite. Probably it lays its eggs in the nests of Fire Finches (page 235). The young birds of the Senegal Combassou look very much like those of the Fire Finches.

FOOD: In captivity the Senegal Combassou should be given a varied diet of grain, foxtail millet, greenstuff, some soft food and insects.

BREEDING: Successful breeding in captivity is rare.

Senegal Combassou

POPULAR NAME: **Queen Whydah**
SCIENTIFIC NAME: *Vidua regia*
FAMILY: Ploceidae (Weaverbirds)
SUB-FAMILY: Viduinae (Whydahs)

This Whydah is 12½″ long (32 cm) in breeding plumage; otherwise it measures 5″ (12 cm). The Queen Whydah lives in the dry thornbush grasslands of the central and western parts of southern Africa, in flocks of 10 to 20 birds. The male bird is polygamous, living with a harem of several wives, and only in the incubating season does he wear the splendid plumage with the 4 long tail feathers. The female lays her eggs in the nest of the Violet-eared Waxbill and the Cordon Bleu (pages 226–227 and 224–225). These birds are aggressive in the mating season.

FOOD: A varied mixture of grain, greenstuff and occasional meal-worms.

BREEDING: In 1967, young Queen Whydahs were successfully reared by Violet-eared Waxbills in a South African aviary.

Queen Whydah

POPULAR NAME: **Paradise Whydah**
SCIENTIFIC NAME: *Steganura paradisea*
FAMILY: Ploceidae (Weaverbirds)
SUB-FAMILY: Viduinae (Whydahs)

Measuring up to 16″ (40 cm) in his breeding plumage (see picture, opposite), this Whydah is found in several sub-species (although some of them are regarded as independent species) over wide territories of Africa south of the Sahara, except in the jungles. The bird prefers grasslands with groups of bushes and trees, in which the Waxbills (pages 215–237) and other host-birds of this nest-parasite live. The male Paradise Whydah—wearing his magnificent plumage only in the mating season—gathers several females about him.

FOOD AND CARE: The Paradise Whydah lives mainly on seeds and insects and should be fed and tended in the same way as the Queen Whydah. It can display the full beauty of its flight only in a big aviary, although its long tail may scare birds of other species which share a home with it.

BREEDING: In aviaries large enough for the Paradise Whydah to fly in, breeding is sometimes successful, but its natural host-birds, whose nests it borrows, must also live in the same aviary.

Paradise Whydah

POPULAR NAME: **Pin-tailed Whydah**
SCIENTIFIC NAME: *Vidua macroura*
FAMILY: Ploceidae (Weaverbirds)
SUB-FAMILY: Viduinae (Whydahs)

Like the Queen Whydah, this mere 5″ (12 cm) bird measures no less than 12½″ (32 cm) in its breeding plumage! The Pin-tailed Whydah lives in the grasslands, savannas, and forest borders of tropical Africa south of the Sahara; but it also visits plantations, towns, and villages. It lives on seeds and insects. In its native haunts, the Pin-tailed Whydah lays its eggs in the nests of the St. Helena Waxbill *(Estrilda astrild)* and probably also in that of the Grey Waxbill (page 217) and other birds of the Waxbill genus.

BREEDING: Breeding is successful only if the host-birds (who must rear the Pin-tailed Whydah's young) are given animal food—chiefly ants' eggs and egg-food—long enough. Keep in mind that, like all the Whydahs, the Pin-tailed Whydah attacks the eggs of other species. Therefore, once it has laid its own eggs, it cannot be kept in an aviary with other breeding birds.

Pin-tailed Whydah

POPULAR NAME: **White-winged Whydah**
SCIENTIFIC NAME: *Euplectes albonotatus**
FAMILY: Ploceidae (Weaverbirds)
SUB-FAMILY: Euplectinae (Whydahs)

Over 6½″ (17 cm) long in its splendid plumage
(illustrated), this Whydah lives in the open grasslands of wide territories extending over eastern,
central and southern Africa. The male assembles
6 to 10 females about him, building a nest for
each of them. During the incubation period he is
quite aggressive. Outside the breeding season, the
plumage of the male is just as undistinguished-
looking as the female's. The White-winged Whydah
likes to be near water and often perches on grass
and seed stalks.

FOOD: In captivity, the White-winged Whydah
should be fed on seeds—chiefly grass seed—and
insects. Tend this bird in the same way as you must
the other whydahs.

BREEDING: If kept in a spacious aviary, the
White-winged Whydah will breed.

*Viduinae and Euplectinae birds are all known
as whydahs.

White-winged Whydah

POPULAR NAMES: **Orange Bishop; Orange Weaver**
SCIENTIFIC NAME: *Euplectes orix franciscanus*
FAMILY: Ploceidae (Weaverbirds)
SUB-FAMILY: Euplectinae (Whydahs)

Two varieties of this 5″ (12 cm) bird exist, and wide areas of the northern parts of western, central and eastern Africa play host to both of them. The Orange Bishop is regarded by many scientists as a sub-species of the Red Bishop or Grenadier Weaver *(Euplectes orix orix)*, which it resembles. The Orange Bishop lives on seeds, insects and wild fruit and plunders cornfields if it can. The male bird keeps a harem of 4 to 5 females. The skilfully woven egg-shaped nest has a covered entrance in its side. The male stands out during breeding time because of his mingled dark and red plumage (see picture, opposite); at other times he is hardly distinguishable from the brownish female. In captivity it unfortunately often happens that the bird has dull orange-yellow feathers instead of red ones.

FOOD: This bird needs a varied diet—a good mixture of cereals supplemented with foxtail-millet seed, fruit, egg-food, ants' eggs, mealworms and the like will help the Orange Bishop to feel at home in captivity. Moreover, such food is essential for preservation of the male's red plumage.

BREEDING: Although industrious nest-builders,

Orange Bishop

even in captivity, these birds do not breed readily in a communal aviary.

POPULAR NAMES: **Fire-crowned Bishop; Crimson-crowned Weaver**

SCIENTIFIC NAME: *Euplectes hordeaceus*

FAMILY: Ploceidae (Weaverbirds)

SUB-FAMILY: Euplectinae (Whydahs)

Several sub-species of this 5″ (13 cm) polygamous Weaver live over much of Africa south of the Sahara. The Fire-crowned Bishop finds its food in marshy areas and in the grasslands bordering rivers. Joining in with Red-billed Queleas, Fire-crowned Bishops often form tremendous flocks. This Weaver suspends its globular nest of fresh grass on 2 vertical twigs, the hen laying 2 to 4 eggs.

FOOD AND CARE: The Fire-crowned Bishop should be given the same kind of food as the other Weavers. Like them, it will feel most at home in an aviary that gives it enough freedom of movement.

BREEDING: Successful breeding in captivity is exceptional.

Fire-crowned Bishop

POPULAR NAMES: **Napoleon Weaver; Golden Bishop; Yellow-crowned Bishop**

SCIENTIFIC NAME: *Euplectes afer*

FAMILY: Ploceidae (Weaverbirds)

SUB-FAMILY: Euplectinae (Whydahs)

A polygamous bird, this $4\frac{1}{2}''$ to $5''$ (11 to 12 cm) Weaver comes in several sub-species that inhabit the grasslands of much of Africa south of the Sahara Desert. It prefers swampy country or places where water is nearby, so it can build its nest—in small colonies—between reeds and other water plants. The Napoleon Weaver lives on seeds and insects. The young birds leave their eggs after 14 days and are fledged 3 weeks later.

FOOD: Feed the Napoleon Weaver in the same way you would the Orange Bishop.

Napoleon Weaver

POPULAR NAMES: **Red-billed Quelea; Red-billed Dioch; Red-billed Weaver**

SCIENTIFIC NAME: *Quelea quelea*
FAMILY: Ploceidae (Weaverbirds)
SUB-FAMILY: Euplectinae (Whydahs)

Africa south of the Sahara—except for the rain forests and deserts—is the home of this bird. The Red-billed Quelea is a bird of the grassland zone, where it frequents swamps. The Red-billed Quelea averages from $4\frac{1}{2}''$ to $5\frac{1}{4}''$ (12 cm) in length and comes in several varieties. The picture, opposite, shows the type found in western Africa. This bird forms gigantic flocks. (As many as 100 million of these birds have been counted in a single flock.) Unlike the Orange Bishop, it breeds in large nesting-colonies, filling the trees with nests. It lays 2 to 4 eggs and feeds chiefly on seeds and insects.

FOOD: The Red-billed Quelea needs the same kinds of food as the Orange Bishop.

BREEDING: Although the Red-billed Quelea is an industrious nest-builder even when it is in captivity, it can seldom be made to breed.

Red-billed Quelea

POPULAR NAMES: **Black-headed Weaver; Village Weaver**

SCIENTIFIC NAME: *Ploceus cucullatus*
FAMILY: Ploceidae (Weaverbirds)
SUB-FAMILY: Ploceinae (True Weavers)

Large areas of western, central and eastern Africa play host to the several sub-species of this 6½″ (17 cm) bird. The sociable Black-headed Weaver lives in savannas, thornbush grasslands, reedy lakes and riversides, and human communities. It forms nesting-colonies high up in the trees. The carefully built nest contains 2 or 3 eggs. The male builds nests for 4 or 5 females and shows his splendid plumage only during the incubation period. The young birds' leave their eggs after 14 days of incubation and fly away 3 weeks later. Seeds of many kinds, insects (including flying termites) and spiders form the natural food of the Black-headed Weaver.

FOOD: In captivity, this bird should be fed with grain, including rice, and with greenstuff, eggs, cheese, and—while it is incubating its eggs, with meal-worms above all else.

BREEDING: The Black-headed Weaver will breed in captivity.

Black-headed Weaver

POPULAR NAMES: **Yellow Masked Weaver; Vitelline
Weaver**
SCIENTIFIC NAME: *Ploceus velatus vitellinus*
FAMILY: Ploceidae (Weaverbirds)
SUB-FAMILY: Ploceinae (True Weavers)

The picture opposite shows the striking black mask
of this yellow bird. The Yellow Masked Weaver
averages 5″ (12 cm) and comes from the seasonally
dry grasslands of Africa; its distribution area
stretches from Senegal to Sudan. It lives on seeds
and insects and also attacks cornfields. Its nests
are often built in small breeding-colonies in the
tops of acacia trees.

FOOD AND CARE: This bird should be tended and
fed in the same way as the Black-headed Weaver.

BREEDING: The Yellow Masked Weaver is a
peace-loving bird that will breed in an aviary.

Yellow Masked Weaver

POPULAR NAMES: **Java Sparrow; Ricebird**
SCIENTIFIC NAME: *Padda oryzivora*
FAMILY: Estrildidae (Weaverfinches)

Originally from Java and Bali, this 5½″ (14 cm) bird in the course of time spread over a territory today covering practically all of southeastern Asia, Indonesia, the Philippines and southern China. It lives in grasslands and farms where there are brushwood and groups of trees and also visits parks and gardens. It lives mainly on rice (it is sometimes called the "Ricebird") and other seeds. The sociable Java Sparrow makes its nest, often in colonies, in trees or tree holes or on buildings. A clutch contains 4 to 7 eggs.

FOOD: In captivity, this bird should be fed with a good mixture of grain; also with rice, greenstuff and—when the young birds are being reared—with ants' eggs.

BREEDING: The Java Sparrow, perhaps the most resistant of the weaverfinches, will breed in an aviary.

Java Sparrow

POPULAR NAME: **Cutthroat**
SCIENTIFIC NAME: *Amadina fasciata*
FAMILY: Estrildidae (Weaverfinches)

About 5″ (12 cm) long, this bird comes in 3 sub-species which inhabit large areas of Africa south of the Sahara, except for the humid rain forests. It feeds on seeds and small insects and often forms gigantic flocks. The bird builds its nest either high in the trees or in the undergrowth, often using the old nests of weaverbirds. The 4 or 5 eggs are incubated by both parents. The young birds leave the eggs after 12 days and fly off 25 days later.

FOOD: It should be fed with millet, foxtail millet, canary seed, semi-ripe grass seed and weed seeds, greenstuff and meal-worms and the like.

BREEDING: In captivity, the Cutthroat can be relied upon to breed in a nesting basket or small nesting box. Often there will be many broods in succession.

Cutthroat

POPULAR NAME: **Indian Silverbill**
SCIENTIFIC NAME: *Euodice malabarica*
FAMILY: Estrildidae (Weaverfinches)

This 4½″ (11½ cm) bird is at home in Ceylon, the Arabian Peninsula and India, where it lives in the grasslands containing groups of bushes and trees, but enjoys visiting fields and gardens. The Indian Silverbill lives on different kinds of seeds and greenstuff. The 4 to 6 eggs are incubated by both parents. The young birds leave the eggs after 11 days and fly off 19 days later.

The Indian Silverbill is closely related to the African Silverbill (see page 193), and many ornithologists regard it and the African Silverbill as sub-species of one and the same species.

FOOD: In addition to a universal grain food, give the Indian Silverbill greenstuff and sprouting spray millet.

BREEDING: The Indian Silverbill will breed in an aviary.

Indian Silverbill

POPULAR NAME: **African Silverbill**
SCIENTIFIC NAME: *Euodice malabarica cantans*
FAMILY: Estrildidae (Weaverfinches)

This handsome songster is very similar to the Indian Silverbill and even approximates it in size (the African Silverbill averages 4" or 4½" (11 cm) in length). The African Silverbill comes from Senegal, Tanzania, parts of northern Africa, and the southwestern parts of the Arabian Peninsula. It prefers grasslands and is fond of having a river nearby; it also visits towns and villages. The African Silverbill makes its nest in dense undergrowth and, like the Indian Silverbill, is a peaceable, lively bird.

FOOD: The African Silverbill needs the same kind of food as the Indian Silverbill.

BREEDING: This petite bird with an attractive song is, above all, a dependable breeder that will rear several broods a year. Like the Bengal Finch *(Lonchura domestica)*, it serves excellently as a nurse for bringing up strange birds.

NOTE: As indicated previously, some ornithologists regard the African Silverbill and the Indian Silverbill as sub-species.

African Silverbill

POPULAR NAME: **Grey-headed Silverbill**
SCIENTIFIC NAME: *Odontospiza caniceps*
FAMILY: Estrildidae (Weaverfinches)

This 4″ (10 cm) Weaverfinch lives in the dry thornbush grasslands of eastern Africa. It feeds mostly on grass seed and small insects. Both sexes have the same coloring, but the male can be recognized by his attractive song. The Grey-headed Silverbill builds its nest generally on the tips of the limbs of medium-sized trees and lays 4 or 5 eggs. This bird has been exported in significant quantities only since 1962.

FOOD: Like all of the weaverfinches, the Grey-headed Silverbill should be fed with a varied mixture of grain and with foxtail millet, unripe grass seed, and greenstuff, supplemented now and then by insects, especially meal-worms.

BREEDING: Animal food is essential for successful breeding.

Grey-headed Silverbill

POPULAR NAME: **White-headed Mannikin**
SCIENTIFIC NAME: *Lonchura maja*
FAMILY: Estrildidae (Weaverfinches)

Two sub-species of this 4″ to 4½″ (approximately 11 cm) Weaverfinch live in the Malay Peninsula and in Sumatra, Java and Bali. The White-headed Mannikin is a bird of the open grasslands, but like the other weaverfinches, is a frequent visitor to rice fields. It lives on grass seed and rice. The White-headed Mannikin builds its ball-shaped nest near the ground in thick grass, brushwood, or low trees. The hen lays 3 to 5 eggs, which are incubated by both parents. The young birds hatch 13 days later and, as fledglings, leave the nest 25 days afterwards.

FOOD: Millet, foxtail millet, canary-grass seed, rice, greenstuff and the like.

BREEDING: The White-headed Mannikin is a friendly bird that is often successfully bred in captivity.

White-headed Mannikin

POPULAR NAME: **Tricolored Mannikin**
SCIENTIFIC NAME: *Lonchura malacca malacca*
FAMILY: Estrildidae (Weaverfinches)

This 4½″ (11 to 12 cm) rice-loving bird belongs to the same species as the equally popular Black-headed Mannikin *(Lonchura malacca atricapilla)*. However, the distribution area of the Tricolored Mannikin extends from eastern India to southern China. It lives in grasslands, reedy marshes and bushland and often invades rice fields and sugar-cane plantations. The bird finds its food—seeds of many kinds including rice—on the ground. The Tricolored Mannikin builds its nest in bushes, undergrowth or trees, the hen laying 4 to 6 eggs.

FOOD AND CARE: In captivity, this bird should be fed like the White-headed Mannikin; but when the Tricolored Mannikin is rearing its young, additional food is advisable. At these times, supplement its regular diet with ants' eggs, meal-worms, and hard-boiled eggs. The aviary or cage should contain vertical stalks and branches. In fact, you should supply these whenever you are raising cage birds that naturally live in reeds and grass.

Tricolored Mannikin

POPULAR NAMES: **Nutmeg Mannikin; Spice Finch;**
Nutmeg Finch

SCIENTIFIC NAME: *Lonchura punctulata*

FAMILY: Estrildidae (Weaverfinches)

The distribution area of this $4\frac{1}{2}''$ (11 to 12 cm)
Weaverfinch ranges from India to southern China,
the Philippines, and the Sunda Islands. It lives in
open country as well as in farmland, gardens and
parks, appearing in great flocks and frequently
visiting rice fields. It feeds on seeds and insects.
The Nutmeg Mannikin builds its nest in thorny
scrub, the hen laying 4 to 7 eggs. The young birds
leave the eggs after 13 days and can fly 3 weeks
later. The Nutmeg Mannikin, a naturally easy-
going bird, soon becomes tame.

FOOD: This bird needs the same kind of food as
the Tricolored Mannikin.

BREEDING: Unfortunately, the Nutmeg Mannikin will not breed readily in captivity.

Nutmeg Mannikin

POPULAR NAME: **Longtailed Grassfinch**
SCIENTIFIC NAME: *Poephila acuticauda*
FAMILY: Estrildidae (Weaverfinches)

The picture (opposite) shows 2 sub-species of this Weaverfinch: the yellow-billed nominal form *acuticauda acuticauda* and the red-billed *acuticauda hecki*. The male Longtailed Grassfinches reach lengths up to $6\frac{1}{2}''$ or $7''$ (17 cm); the female is rather smaller. The Longtailed Grassfinch is at home in the grasslands of northern Australia. It is fond of areas where there is water nearby and lives on grass seed, other kinds of seeds, and small insects. The bird builds its nest either high up in trees and bushes or low in the grass; the clutch contains 5 or 6 eggs.

FOOD: In captivity, feed this bird on grain, some soft food, insects and greenstuff.

BREEDING: The Longtailed Grassfinch breeds readily in captivity.

Longtailed Grassfinch

POPULAR NAME: **Gouldian Finch**
SCIENTIFIC NAME: *Erythrura gouldiae*
FAMILY: Estrildidae (Weaverfinches)

The hot savannas of northern Australia are home to this 5″ (12 to 13 cm) bird which comes in three varieties: a black-headed variety, a red-headed variety (illustrated)—and also a very rare yellow-headed variety. The Gouldian Finch displays a preference for open bush and grasslands near water and for mangrove forests. It finds its food on the ground, but builds its nest in trees or in natural tree holes or termite holes. A clutch contains 5 to 8 eggs. The young birds leave the eggs after about 16 days and the nest, 24 or 25 days later. The Gouldian Finch is a sociable bird.

FOOD: In captivity, feed this bird with canary-grass seed, foxtail millet, unripe grass-panicles, and green plants.

BREEDING: The warmth-loving Gouldian Finch will breed in a box in a canary-cage if it is given proper care.

Gouldian Finch

POPULAR NAMES: **Tricolored Parrot Finch; Blue-faced Parrot Finch; Three-colored Parrot Finch**

SCIENTIFIC NAME: *Erythrura trichroa*

FAMILY: Estrildidae (Weaverfinches)

The several sub-species of this $4\frac{1}{2}''$ (11 to 12 cm) bird all live in Indonesia and other islands of the Pacific Ocean and in northeastern Australia, as well as in New Guinea and many islands in the Indian Ocean. The birds live in pairs in coastal forests, in forest clearings and on plantations, where they find most of their food: seeds and insects. The Tricolored Parrot Finch builds its nest concealed in undergrowth, or in rock crevices. A clutch contains 3 to 6 eggs, which are incubated for 12 or 13 days.

FOOD: In captivity, seeds soaked in water, foxtail millet, canary-grass seed, hemp, soft food, ants' eggs, meal-worms and greenstuff.

BREEDING: Experienced bird-keepers will find that they can get the Tricolored Parrot Finch to breed in captivity.

Tricolored Parrot Finch

POPULAR NAME: **Pin-tailed Nonpareil**
SCIENTIFIC NAME: *Erythrura prasina*
FAMILY: Estrildidae (Weaverfinches)

Borneo, Indo-China, Sumatra and Java play host to the 2 sub-species of this lively $4\frac{1}{2}''$ to $5\frac{1}{2}''$ (12 to 14 cm) bird. The Pin-tailed Nonpareil prefers forest borders with plenty of bushes and the rice fields that adjoin such areas in its native parts of the world. This bird looks for its food—seeds (mainly rice) and small insects—on the ground.

FOOD: Newly imported Pin-tailed Nonpareils have to make do with unhusked rice. But in the community aviary they soon learn to appreciate other grain-food. In its natural haunts, the friendly Pin-tailed Nonpareil makes its nest in dense undergrowth. The female is somewhat more plainly colored than the male shown in the picture (opposite).

BREEDING: Unfortunately this handsome bird seldom breeds in captivity.

Pin-tailed Nonpareil

Living mainly on grass seed, this 4″ to 4½″ (10 to 11 cm) bird and many of its varieties are among the most popular, toughest, and easiest-to-breed of the weaverfinches. The type in this picture comes from Australia, while another variety (looking much like the Australian birds). lives in some of the smaller Sunda Islands. The Zebra Finch is a bird of the open grasslands endowed with scattered groups of bushes and trees. It forms great flocks in grassland areas where water is nearby, and makes small nesting-colonies in the undergrowth and in many other places. A clutch contains 4 to 6 eggs.

FOOD: In captivity this bird should be fed with a good mixture of grain and with foxtail millet and green food.

BREEDING: If given a nesting basket or nesting box in captivity, the Zebra Finch will make a nest inside its cage.

Zebra Finch

POPULAR NAME: **Diamond Sparrow**
SCIENTIFIC NAME: *Stagonopleura guttata*
FAMILY: Estrildidae (Weaverfinches)

About $4\frac{1}{2}''$ (approximately 11 cm) long, this sociable and lively bird is a creature of eastern Australia's open grasslands wherever interspersed groups of bushes and trees can also be found. The Diamond Sparrow finds its food—chiefly grass seed, but also small insects—on the ground. Except at breeding time, the bird flies in small flocks. The closed nest is often built in small colonies in bushes and trees. The 5 to 7 eggs are incubated for 12 days, and the young birds are fledged 3 weeks later.

FOOD: The Diamond Sparrow eats the same kind of food as the Longtailed Grassfinch.

BREEDING: In captivity this Weaverfinch will readily breed in its wooden nesting box in an aviary. But remember, as a sociable bird, the Diamond Sparrow thrives best in a big aviary.

Diamond Sparrow

POPULAR NAME: **Orange-cheeked Waxbill**
SCIENTIFIC NAME: *Estrilda melpoda*
FAMILY: Estrildidae (Weaverfinches)

Western and central Africa are the home territory of this 4″ (10 cm) bird, which usually lives near water and looks for the seeds and insects that are its food on the ground or in tall grass. Except in the incubating season, it forms quite large flocks. The Orange-cheeked Waxbill makes its bottle-shaped nest on the ground, concealed by grass. It lays 4 to 6 eggs which are incubated for 12 days. The young birds can fly 3 weeks later.

FOOD: The Orange-cheeked Waxbill should be fed on foxtail and ordinary millet, canary seed, grass seed, soft food, and greenstuff. Add egg-food, ants' eggs and fruit flies when the bird is incubating.

BREEDING: In captivity, the Orange-cheeked Waxbill is most likely to breed if kept in a well-planted aviary. It does not like being disturbed.

Orange-cheeked Waxbill

POPULAR NAMES: **Grey Waxbill; Pink-cheeked
Waxbill**
SCIENTIFIC NAME: *Estrilda troglodytes*
FAMILY: Estrildidae (Weaverfinches)

Only 3½" to 4" (9 to 10 cm) long, this friendly bird
lives in the seasonally arid steppelike country of
western and northeastern Africa, mainly frequenting swampy districts, grasslands and groups
of bushes, as well as agricultural land. Forming
small flocks, it feeds on seeds and insects. The Grey
Waxbill builds its arched nest, which sometimes
contains a separate "bedroom," on the ground in
the grass or in low thorn scrub. It lays 2 to 6 eggs.
The young Grey Waxbills leave the eggs after 11
days and can fly 3 weeks later.

FOOD: Feed the Grey Waxbill in the same way
as you would the Orange-cheeked Waxbill, but
add plenty of animal food when the bird is
incubating.

BREEDING: This friendly bird will breed in captivity.

Grey Waxbill

POPULAR NAMES: **Star Finch; Red-tailed Grassfinch;**
Ruficauda Finch
SCIENTIFIC NAME: *Bathilda ruficauda*
FAMILY: Estrildidae (Weaverfinches)

This denizen of northern Australia (4″ to 4½″;
11 cm) lives in reedy river banks and grassland,
feeding on seeds and insects. The Star Finch
builds its well-concealed bag-shaped nest in tall
grass, undergrowth, or low trees. It lays 3 or 4
eggs, which are incubated for 12 or 13 days. The
young birds fledge 3 weeks after hatching.

FOOD AND CARE: The warmth-loving Star Finch,
a friendly bird, should be tended in the same way
as the Orange-cheeked Waxbill.

BREEDING: Experience has proved that breeding
prospects are best if the bird is kept in an aviary,
and additional animal food should be added when
it is bringing up its youngsters.

Star Finch

POPULAR NAMES: **Lavender Finch; Lavender Waxbill**
SCIENTIFIC NAME: *Estrilda caerulescens*
FAMILY: Estrildidae (Weaverfinches)

A denizen of tropical western Africa, this 4″ to 4½″ (11 cm) bird lives—in small communities—in grassy districts, bushland, and forest borders. Like the other weaverfinches, it finds its food—insects and seeds—on the ground and is not afraid of any nearby humans. The Lavender Finch builds its ball-shaped nest in the undergrowth, and both parents incubate the 3 or 4 eggs for 12 days.

FOOD: This bird should be tended and fed in the same way as the Orange-cheeked Waxbill, but needs a bigger proportion of living insects when bringing up its young.

BREEDING: In captivity, the Lavender Finch is most likely to breed in a well-planted aviary.

Lavender Finch

POPULAR NAME: **Blue-headed Waxbill**
SCIENTIFIC NAME: *Uraeginthus cyanocephalus*
FAMILY: Estrildidae (Weaverfinches)

Tanzania, Kenya and Ethiopia are the home territory of this $4\frac{1}{2}''$ (12 cm) inhabitant of the arid grasslands of eastern Africa. The Blue-headed Waxbill finds its food—seeds and insects—on the ground. It is more sensitive to damp and cold than the Cordon Bleu. The Blue-headed Waxbill builds its nest, an egg-shaped structure with a side entrance, in brushwood. Both the parents incubate the 3 or 4 eggs.

FOOD: The Blue-headed Waxbill should be fed with a varied assortment of grain and with foxtail millet, grass-panicles, greenstuff, and—particularly when brooding—insects.

BREEDING: This bird will breed in captivity and will accept a small basket or nest box as a foundation for the nest it must build.

Blue-headed Waxbill

POPULAR NAME: **Cordon Bleu**
SCIENTIFIC NAME: *Uraeginthus bengalus*
FAMILY: Estrildidae (Weaverfinches)

This 4½″ (12 cm) Weaverfinch (in its 9 sub-species) inhabits great parts of northern tropical Africa. The Cordon Bleu is a bird of the grasslands containing scattered, thorny scrub. It looks for its food—seeds, termites and other insects—on the ground, in pairs or small flocks. Often these will enter populated places and use their water supplies. The Cordon Bleu builds its spherical nest in a well-protected position inside thornbushes. Both parents incubate the 3 to 6 eggs for about 11 days.

FOOD: The Cordon Bleu should be given the same kind of food as the Blue-headed Waxbill. It feeds its young almost exclusively on insects.

BREEDING: This bird will breed in a room or a well-planted aviary. Remember that the Cordon Bleu loves warmth and needs plenty of flying space.

Cordon Bleu

POPULAR NAME: **Violet-eared Waxbill**
SCIENTIFIC NAME: *Uraeginthus granatinus*
FAMILY: Estrildidae (Weaverfinches)

Another warmth-loving bird, this Weaverfinch from southern Africa averages $5\frac{1}{2}''$ (14 cm). It lives in grasslands with thorny bush, like the closely related Cordon Bleu. The Violet-eared Waxbill feeds on seeds and insects. The bird builds its ball-shaped nest, made of grass, in rigid, thorny bushes offering good protection. The 3 or 4 eggs are incubated for 13 days, and the young birds leave the nest 16 days later. The Queen Whydah illustrated on page 167 lays her eggs in the Violet-eared Waxbill's nest.

FOOD AND CARE: This warmth-loving bird should be fed in the same way as the Cordon Bleu, although with a larger share of insects and soft food. Like the Cordon Bleu, it needs plenty of flying space.

BREEDING: The Violet-eared Waxbill rarely breeds in captivity.

Violet-eared Waxbill

SCIENTIFIC NAME: *Amandava amandava*
FAMILY: Estrildidae (Weaverfinches)

Three sub-species of this Weaverfinch live in a territory extending from India through Indo-China to Indonesia. Averaging 4″ (10 cm), this bird inhabits grassy country, marshes, bushwoods and farms, feeding on grass seed and insects. It is a friendly, good-natured bird and has a pleasant song. The Amadavat builds its nest in dense scrub, the hen laying 4 to 7 eggs. The male bird is the only one of the weaverfinches to change his plumage at breeding time, when he looks very splendid (see picture, opposite); at other times he is almost indistinguishable from the plain female.

FOOD: The Amadavat needs the same diet as the Cordon Bleu.

BREEDING: This friendly songster breeds readily.

Amadavat

POPULAR NAME: **Melba Finch**
SCIENTIFIC NAME: *Pytilia melba*
FAMILY: Estrildidae (Weaverfinches)

Wide areas of Africa south of the Sahara Desert play host to the 7 different sub-species of this bird. The Melba Finch averages $4\frac{1}{2}''$ to $5''$ (12 to 13 cm) and inhabits the seasonally arid grasslands that are endowed with thorny scrub. Except in the breeding season, it forms small flocks in these grasslands together with the Cordon Bleu and the Fire Finch. The Melba Finch searches the ground for the grass seeds and small insects it feeds on and builds its nest in low thornbushes. The 3 to 5 eggs are incubated for 13 days. The young birds, which are fed almost exclusively on insects, fly 3 weeks after leaving the eggs.

FOOD: This bird needs the same diet as the Cordon Bleu.

BREEDING: The Melba Finch will breed in captivity—even in a nesting box if there is no brushwood handy.

Melba Finch

POPULAR NAME: **Peter's Twin-spot**
SCIENTIFIC NAME: *Hypargos niveoguttatus*
FAMILY: Estrildidae (Weaverfinches)

Eastern Africa is the home of this warmth-loving
bird. There it lives hidden by dense brushwood in
vegetation that fringes water, and in the undergrowth of forest borders. Peter's Twin-spot, $4\frac{1}{2}''$ to
$5''$ in length (11 to 12 cm) feeds on various seeds
and insects, building its ball-shaped nest not far
above ground-level in the brushwood. The 3 to 6
eggs are incubated by both parents. The young
birds hatch after 12 days of incubating and are
fledged 3 weeks later.

FOOD: Feed this bird with varied kinds of millet
including foxtail millet, and with grass seed,
canary-grass seed, sprouting seeds, packaged soft
food, ants' eggs, and living insects.

BREEDING: Peter's Twin-spot breeds in captivity.
Remember that it likes warmth.

Peter's Twin-spot

POPULAR NAME: **Fire Finch**
SCIENTIFIC NAME: *Lagonosticta senegala*
FAMILY: Estrildidae (Weaverfinches)

Western, central and eastern Africa play host to this 4″ (10 cm) Weaverfinch, which comes in several sub-species. The Fire Finch inhabits grassland scattered with dense scrub, but is not afraid to venture out into populated districts and to mingle with domestic poultry. It often joins flocks of other weaverfinches and, in captivity, has shown itself to be resistant, friendly and tame. The Fire Finch finds its food, chiefly seeds, on the ground. It builds its nest either in the grass, in brushwood, or under projecting roof edges. A clutch contains 4 or 5 eggs. The young birds hatch after 11 or 12 days and are fledged 18 days later. The Senegal Combassou (page 165) lays its eggs into the Fire Finch's nest.

FOOD: Feed your Fire Finch in the same way you would the Orange-cheeked Waxbill (page 214).

BREEDING: In captivity, this hardy, easily tamed bird breeds readily.

Fire Finch

POPULAR NAMES: **Aurora Waxbill; Aurora Finch**
SCIENTIFIC NAME: *Pytilia phoenicoptera*
FAMILY: Estrildidae (Weaverfinches)

Several sub-species of this $4\frac{1}{2}''$ to $5\frac{1}{2}''$ (11 to 12 cm) bird inhabit western and eastern Africa. The picture (opposite) shows the red-billed variety *(lineata)* from Ethiopia: that is, the Striped Aurora Waxbill. The other varieties have a black bill. The Aurora Waxbill lives in dry forests and bush and in agricultural land. It feeds on seeds and insects and—outside of the breeding season—seldom visits the ground. The Aurora Waxbill builds its nest in dense undergrowth with the hen laying 4 eggs. It is a friendly and good-tempered bird.

FOOD: In addition to the usual Weaverfinch diet, this bird needs insects and soft food; the young are fed almost entirely with insects.

Aurora Waxbill

POPULAR NAMES: **Talking Mynah, Hill Mynah**
SCIENTIFIC NAME: *Gracula religiosa*
FAMILY: Sturnidae (Starlings)

Its extraordinary talents as an imitator make this bird one of the most interesting of all cage birds. It wonderfully mimics human speech as skilfully as it can sing melodies it has heard. The Talking Mynah comes in 11 sub-species, whose lengths vary from $9\frac{1}{2}''$ (24 cm) to $12''$ (30 cm). Some kinds live in pairs—others, in flocks of 20 to 30 birds. All frequent jungles and bamboo thickets; in many districts these birds also visit populated areas. The native territory of this bird extends from Ceylon and India to Hainan Island in the South China Sea and Indonesia.

The Talking Mynah feeds on fruit, flower nectar and many kinds of insects. It builds its nest in natural tree holes or in nesting holes that have been abandoned, by woodpeckers. The clutch contains 2 eggs.

FOOD AND CARE: Feed the Talking Mynah on packaged soft food, meal-worms, raw minced meat, and fruit. Keep a watch, as it will steal from other nests if kept in a community aviary. A tame Talking Mynah can be allowed to fly about, but—you have been warned!—being a softbilled bird, its habits are not very tidy.

BREEDING: In captivity, breeding is rarely

Talking Mynah

successful even if the birds are kept in a large aviary.

POPULAR NAME: **Bank Mynah**
SCIENTIFIC NAME: *Acridotheres ginginianus*
FAMILY: Sturnidae (Starlings)

This 8″ to 8½″ (approximately 21 cm) Mynah has, like the Indian House Mynah, become thoroughly domesticated. Everywhere in its native territory—in railroad depots, in villages, among boats, on refuse dumps, in pastures—it can be seen searching for insects and left-over food. The Bank Mynah makes its nest in holes it excavates by the banks of rivers or under bridges. India and parts of southern Asia are its home.

FOOD: The Bank Mynah needs the same diet as the Talking Mynah. It feeds its young with living food.

BREEDING: In captivity, this bird will breed in a nesting box.

Bank Mynah

POPULAR NAME: **Pagoda Starling**
SCIENTIFIC NAME: *Sturnus pagodarum*
FAMILY: Sturnidae (Starlings)

The distribution area of this 8″ (20 cm) bird extends from Afghanistan to India, Nepal and Ceylon. It lives in open country, but visits villages. It is a good mimic and a popular household pet in its native territories. The Pagoda Starling lives on wild berries, figs and insects. It breeds in hollow trees or (less frequently) uses holes in walls. The 3 or 4 eggs are incubated by both parents.

FOOD: Packaged universal soft food, fruit, white bread soaked in milk and egg-food.

BREEDING: The Pagoda Starling often breeds in captivity.

Pagoda Starling

POPULAR NAMES: **Superb Glossy Starling; Spreo**
Starling
SCIENTIFIC NAME: *Spreo superbus*
FAMILY: Sturnidae (Starlings)

Southeastern Sudan, southern Ethiopia, and
Tanzania are the native territory of this 8″ to 8½″
bird (approximately 21 cm) whose plumage
gleams metallically in the sunshine. It can be seen
in great numbers in pastures, fields, gardens and
villages, feeding mainly on insects. The Superb
Glossy Starling builds its nest either in brush or in
holes in trees and rocks. It lays 4 eggs.

FOOD: Feed the Superb Glossy Starling with
packaged universal softbill food and with fly-
maggots, ants' eggs, raw meat, meal-worms, and
earthworms.

BREEDING: This rather quarrelsome, yet quite
friendly, bird will breed freely in a sufficiently
roomy aviary—provided it gets the food it needs.

Superb Glossy Starling

An endangered species, this 10″ (25 cm) bird is found only in northwestern Bali. It can be seen in many zoos, but is seldom privately owned. It appears in small flocks and builds its nest in tree holes. As a rule, the Bali Mynah lays 3 eggs. It lives chiefly on fruit and is particularly fond of papayas.

FOOD: In captivity, the Bali Mynah should be given soft food, fruits, insects, meal-worms, and other insect larvae.

NOTE: Ensuring the survival of this rare bird is an important part of nature-conservation activities in the zoological gardens of the world.

Bali Mynah

POPULAR NAME: **Royal Starling**
SCIENTIFIC NAME: *Cosmopsarus regius*
FAMILY: Sturnidae (Starlings)

This $13\frac{1}{2}''$ to 14″ (34 to 35 cm) Starling lives in small flocks in the acacia-tree-dotted grasslands of eastern Africa, from southern Ethiopia to Mount Kilimanjaro. It lives on fruit, insects and seeds and lays its 3 or 4 eggs in tree holes. The eggs are incubated by the female alone, but the young birds are brought up by both parents.

FOOD AND CARE: The Royal Starling should be fed on universal food, many meal-worms, raw meat, ants' eggs, insects, fruit, white bread soaked in milk and grated carrots. Ants' eggs and meal-worms are preferred as food when the young birds are being reared. Because of its long tail the Royal Starling needs a big aviary.

BREEDING: It is quite possible to make the bird breed in captivity if it has plenty of flying room.

Royal Starling

POPULAR NAME: **Jackdaw**
SCIENTIFIC NAME: *Corvus monedula*
FAMILY: Corvidae (Crows)

Boasting an average size of 13″ (33 cm), this bird lives all over Europe except for the extreme northern regions of that continent. It is also native to northwestern Africa and to parts of temperate Asia. In all these places, the Jackdaw inhabits rock gorges, parks and farmland, appearing in the wintertime in fields and on refuse heaps. The Jackdaw breeds in rock crevices, towers, holes in walls and hollow trees. It lays 3 to 6 eggs which are incubated for 16 to 19 days. The young birds are fledged 30 to 35 days afterwards. The Jackdaw eats anything going, but prefers snails, mice, insects, and worms.

FOOD AND CARE: In captivity, the Jackdaw's preference is for left-over food of all kinds. These birds can be kept in a room or a big aviary, and jackdaw nestlings will become very tame.

Jackdaw

POPULAR NAME: **Nutcracker**
SCIENTIFIC NAME: *Nucifraga caryocatactes*
FAMILY: Corvidae (Crows)

Existing in several sub-species, this approximately
12½″ long (32 cm) bird has a preference for moder-
ately high mountainous areas—and a widespread
distribution, too: the suitably mountainous regions
of central and eastern Europe, southern Scandi-
navia, northeastern Europe, large parts of Siberia
as far as Korea, and Japan and the Himalayas.
The Siberian sub-species of the Nutcracker sometimes appears in Europe in great numbers in the
winter. A bird of the northern evergreen forests,
the Nutcracker builds its nest in coniferous trees.
It lays 3 or 4 eggs which are incubated for 17 to
19 days.

FOOD: The Nutcracker feeds chiefly on nuts,
tree seeds, insects and fruit.

BREEDING: The breeding activity of this bird
has been less researched than that of many exotic
birds—an interesting reason for keeping it.

Nutcracker

INDEX

INDEX TO POPULAR NAMES